All Things New

Finding New Life Through Forgiveness

by Cheryl Braden

All Things New

All Scripture quotations, unless otherwise indicated, are taken from The Holy Bible, New International Version®, NIV® Copyright © 1973, 1978, 1984, 2011 by Biblica, Inc.® Used by permission of Zondervan. All rights reserved worldwide. www.Zondervan.com. Scripture taken from *THE MESSAGE*. Copyright © 1993, 1994, 1995, 1996, 2000, 2001, 2002. Used by permission of NavPress Publishing Group.

Paperback ISBN 978-1-959887-00-3
eBook ISBN 978-1-959887-01-0

Copyright © 2022 by Cheryl Braden

All rights reserved. No portion of this book may be reproduced in any form without written permission from the publisher or author, except as permitted by U.S. copyright law.

Library of Congress Control Number: 2022922861

Printed in the United States of America

First Edition 2022

Published by Legacy Inc
P.O. Box 4228
Visalia, CA 93278
www.LegacyInc.org

To my best friend, soulmate, ministry partner, adventure sidekick, love of my life and the best editor ever – Scott James Braden. This book would not exist without you. Your continued encouragement, support and steadfast editing skills have brought this dream to fruition. Thank you for being my forever person.

To my greatest gifts, Micah, Hannah, Cody, Aspen and Remi – my adult children and granddaughters. My love for you is greater than you will ever know. I will forever be your greatest fan.

And to my Lord and Savior, Jesus Christ. There are no words to adequately describe your greatness. I am overwhelmed by your unconditional love, grace and mercy. I am forever committed to you, yearning for the day I see you face to face. Thank you for setting me free!

Contents

Preface	VII
Introduction	VIII
SECTION 1: The Human Journey	1
1. The Lie	2
2. Brokenness	14
3. Intervention	25
SECTION 2: Forgiveness from God	33
4. The Reality	34
5. The Redemption	46
6. The Restoration	56
SECTION 3: Forgiveness Involving Others	71
7. Christ's Model for Forgiveness	72
8. Forgiving Others	87
9. Seeking Forgiveness from Others	111
SECTION 4: Forgiveness and You	127

10.	Forgiving Yourself	128
11.	Truth Over Feelings	140
12.	The New You	157
Afterword		182
The Most Important Decision		184
Endnotes		190
About Author		192

Preface

"The thief comes only to steal and kill and destroy;

I have come that they may have life, and have it to the full."

~Jesus Christ~

John 10:10

Introduction

> *"Forget the former things; do not dwell on the past. See, I am doing **a new thing**! Now it springs up; do you not perceive it? I am making a way in the wilderness and streams in the wasteland."*
> Isaiah 43:18-19

I invite you to **a new thing**. A thing that is right in front of all of us. It's a thing that God knew we would all be destined to experience. In fact, it's more than just **a new thing**. It's an invitation to a new life. A life where past hurts are healed, tragedies are triumphed over and one's soul is set free.

You may be at a place in your life where you've become extremely disappointed. Maybe your life has brought you to a place of great frustration, anger, depression or even hopelessness. Maybe you're drowning in the consequences and realities of past hurts. Maybe your future looks more like a continuation of your painful past. Maybe your life struggles keep revealing issues of unforgiveness.

Life is complicated. It's messy. Our journeys are often weary and burdensome. Desperately wanting things to be different, to feel different and wanting to live different, yet we find ourselves dwelling in the land of former things—and unforgiveness seems to be the biggest giant in the land. If this is you, then I invite you to find a quiet spot and read the pages of *All Things New*.

I invite you to explore what forgiveness is, the power of forgiveness and the idea of forgiving oneself. What does the Bible actually say about all of these? Allow the Lord to do **a new thing** in your life—where you can walk in freedom and in the power of forgiveness.

> *"He who was seated on the throne said, 'I am making everything new!' Then he said, 'Write this down, for these words are trustworthy and true.'"*
> Revelation 21:5

SECTION ONE
The Human Journey

Chapter One
The Lie

It was an early morning run on the treadmill at the gym, and I found my gaze drawn to a figure outside of the window. I watched as a young woman in her twenties held up a sign at the intersection. She was asking people for money. My initial instinct was to not think too deeply about her situation because I knew that the community's nonprofits and services were available.

Yet, this time was different. Something was compelling me. I couldn't get her out of my mind. The more I thought about the situation, the more my heart pounded. I knew then that I needed to speak with her.

As I kept running, I made a deal with God. "God," I said, "if my feelings are true, and you're really wanting me to speak to that young woman, then I'll throw out a fleece. If she's still there at the end of my run, then I'll speak to her. I hope that's good with you. Amen."

Honestly, I was hoping she was gone by the end of my run. It's embarrassing to admit. As the treadmill counted down the last remaining minutes, and then seconds, the woman was still there. I knew I had to initiate a conversation. I had no idea what to say, or how to go about it.

As I left the gym, I noticed a coffee shop in the near distance. I looked at her again as my heart was pounding. I observed her to be younger than I originally thought. I felt an assurance rising in me as I got closer. When I finally was near her, I said softly, with a smile on my face, "Would you like to have a cup of coffee with me? My treat." A long pause ensued, but in a tone of hesitancy she whispered, "Sure."

The two of us walked to the coffee shop together. We placed our orders, I paid the bill, and we sat down in a quaint corner. I told her my name, initiated some small talk and began to ask about her life. Her name was Sophia.

Sophia told me about her parents, that they were good people, but that they were very strict when she was growing up. After graduating high school, Sophia had met Luke at a party and it was an immediate connection. He made her feel loved. He understood her. In just a matter of weeks they both decided to run off together and make a life for themselves.

I interjected as she spoke. "Sophia, how are things going with you and Luke right now?" Immediately, Sophia's face changed. It was almost as if she forced a smile. Then, with pain in her eyes, she admitted things were sort of rough at the moment. She continued, "Luke means well, but sometimes his anger gets the best of him. Things are tight financially so Luke lets several people live with us. People that I don't feel safe with."

Sophia cleared her throat. Tears began. I reached over to give her a hug and gently asked, "Are you okay?" That was all it took. The dam broke and she began to sob. I moved my chair next to hers and handed her some tissue. I just let her cry. After awhile Sophia whispered, "It wasn't supposed to have turned out like this. I had so many plans. I should have known better. How is this my life?"

As the conversation proceeded, Sophia revealed that she had been raised in a family who believed in God, but there had been a time where she began to question all she had been taught. She acknowledged she felt more free when she was younger but that today she was overwhelmed and confused. Life was so uncertain for Sophia.

My heart broke for her. She carried the weight of the world, and she walked in devastating brokenness. I yearned for her to see that God could make all things new. That with God, all things are new!

The human journey carries with it moments in time where we either choose to follow the standards God has set before us, or we choose to alter course and decide for ourselves. It usually begins with thoughts of doubt about the nature of God and His goodness to us. Truly, it all started in the Garden of Eden with one simple question.

Did God really say?

This was literally the exact question posed by the enemy of our souls at the onset of Creation, and he's still asking it of us today. His strategies are not new. It's a simple question elicited by the enemy, and then he watches the seed of doubt take root. It's quite devastating.

Let's look closely into the Genesis 3:1-6 passage to see this process.

> Now the serpent was more crafty than any of the wild animals the Lord God had made. He said to the woman, "Did God really say, 'You must not eat from any tree in the garden'?"
>
> The woman said to the serpent, "We may eat fruit from the trees in the garden, but God did say, 'You must not eat fruit from the tree that is in the middle of the garden, and you

> must not touch it, or you will die.'"
>
> "You will not certainly die," the serpent said to the woman.
>
> "For God knows that when you eat from it your eyes will be opened, and you will be like God, knowing good and evil."
>
> When the woman saw that the fruit of the tree was good for food and pleasing to the eye, and also desirable for gaining wisdom, she took some and ate it. She also gave some to her husband, who was with her, and he ate it.

And so, humanity fell! The great deceiver and enemy of our souls had approached Eve in slithering style and subtlety. He gestured, nodded and questioned with great deception. In just these four words—"Did God really say?"—everything changed.

Eve chose to believe the lie. She chose her own inclinations instead of choosing to believe God at His word. Would you like to know what determines the trajectory of our lives? It's simple. It's how we answer the question, "Did God really say?"

Eve, tell the enemy the truth! Shout it out loud! Say, "Yes, God did say! I trust Him! I trust His word! I trust the boundaries He put in my life! I trust His guidance even though I may not always understand!"

But Eve didn't respond as such, and the perfect world she lived in would quickly disappear. Today, we all live in this fallen state and in this broken world. Why? Because there are severe consequences to disobedience and believing the enemy's lies. Today's choices will always become tomorrow's realities, and we don't have any control of the consequences.

So why do we doubt and question? Why do we incline our hearts to choose what feels right for the moment rather than trust God's directive to not "eat of the fruit of good and evil?" Is it that we don't know God's Word and we'd rather create our own truth? Or is it that we don't trust Him to be good, or trust His rules to govern our lives so that we can experience true joy and fulfillment?

Satan will always attempt to divide us from God, for division is the essence of his relationship with God. In fact, it's his character. Satan chose to separate from God, but he didn't have control of his consequences. Only God did. And forever, the enemy will remain in a blasphemous state, eternally separated from God. And this is precisely the enemy's plan for mankind—that we would rebel in like fashion.

Here are some of the enemy's lies that travel through our minds. They sound like...

- It's your own life.

- Make your own choices.

- Take control of things.

- Do what you want.

- Does God really have your best interest in mind?

- Does He really care about you?

- Is He listening to your prayers?

- Is He really concerned about the hardship you're currently enduring?

- He knows you struggle, so why doesn't He remove this temptation?

- If you want it, take it.

- Don't wait, you might miss out.

- Did God really say?

Satan's skillful suggestions and subtle lies are manipulative, undermining and downright evil. He attempts to influence us to believe that walking apart from God's truth would be better for us. He entices us to believe our current situation isn't so good and that we need to take control of it right away. He tells us to do what is convenient and desirable. He provokes, accuses and creates doubt. And when we take the bait and fall to temptation, everything changes.

When Satan tempted Eve to sin, he made it look appealing to her. He found an area in her life that was weak and susceptible, and fed her lies. She bought the lies. Sin always looks appealing at first. Nobody would take the bait if it wasn't appealing, but it's always a false appeal. The good that sin promises never satisfies. Destruction and insatiability are always produced. The enemy whispers, "Isn't God so limiting?"

Satan always deceives us to part from God's best intentions and beautiful plans. He suggests that our God is controlling and irrelevant; that God's standards will not satisfy nor make us happy. But Satan is the father of lies. Lies are his language and deception his modus operandi. Satan can't force us to sin, but he sure can influence our choices. This is where we must be a student of God's Word, trust in His standards, and walk in faith and victory through obedience.

At first, sin looks so very appealing and enjoyable to us, but after the bite, sin's realization becomes the horror that befalls us. Pain, guilt, shame and loneliness separate us from Him. When we take God from His rightful place and replace His truth with our own answer for truth, then we walk in the deathly consequences of sin.

Again, here's the playbook. Satan gets us to question God. Just like he pressed Eve and asked if it was really a sin (i.e., "Did God really say?"). He twists the motive of God and hints that God was really trying to keep Eve from experiencing the knowledge and power of God. He doesn't stop. He continues to minimize the stated consequence of God's boundary and compels Eve to see the outcome to be something that would give her great advantage and benefit. Ultimately, the enemy shames Eve, condemns her and repeats in unrelenting fashion. Nothing new here. It's still the same for you and me.

Justifying decisions never end well. We should hear a spiritual alarm bell whenever we find ourselves having to justify and create a case for what we want to do. This is always a pivotal moment. We shouldn't have to justify what we're doing. If we are, it most likely means we've walked away, or are walking away, from God's standards — and the results are never good, nor are they life-giving and peaceful.

Here is some more of the enemy's playbook. The enemy twists the truth and creates a false narrative. He repudiates any danger in our false beliefs, and in fact, applauds us and affirms us to move forward with deceptive thinking. We fall into the trap of believing we have the wisdom to make our decisions apart from God and that we will get the favorable outcome we desire. This fallacy leaves us painfully awakened when we experience the consequences of our sin. But we don't stop there. We beat ourselves up. We rehearse, "How could I have fallen for that lie? How can God ever forgive me?" And the enemy is right there shaming us as he feeds us such precise words. He's the one that influenced us to sin, and then he condemns us for doing so. He's such a shameful, blasphemous enemy!

Sin always starts with us questioning God's truth because of the enemy's lies, and ultimately ends with us being separated from God. Temptation and deception often come in the form of a friendly suggestion or a subtle trick. It encourages us to believe something isn't true. More times than not, it comes in our most vulnerable moment and to our greatest weakness. The lie breeds discontentment. It implies God is keeping something good from us. Then, we believe that we have every right to our desires, that somehow our lives would be better if we did things our way instead of God's.

Proverbs 3:5-6 states, "Trust in the Lord with all your heart and lean not on your own understanding; in all your ways submit to Him and He will make your paths straight."

We all have the freedom to choose, but we don't have the freedom to choose our consequences. Our choices will determine our today and tomorrow. After reading this introductory chapter, it's quite possible you're beginning to revisit some sadness and regretful areas from your past or in your life. Please take heart. God's love and pursuit for us has never wavered nor is it going to. We're all on a love journey. In the next chapters we will delve deep into His unrelenting love, redemption and restoration. Please keep reading, and remember, He makes *all things new!*

Reflection Questions and Action Steps:

1. Describe areas in your life where you've been tempted with the question, "Did God really say?"

2. What specific nontruths have you believed only later to realize you've been deceived?

3. How do believing lies from the enemy affect your relationship with God? With others?

4. Consequences of sin are debilitating. What consequence and/or emotional struggle are you currently facing in which you are needing God's healing power?

5. What is the greatest lie you've ever believed and/or have struggled to overcome?

Chapter Two

Brokenness

For years, I've had a dream of visiting Italy. It's one of those countries that beckons you to explore and experience its rich history and romantic culture. This past year, the trip came to fruition. It was an amazing expedition, and it didn't let me down in the least. It was even better than what I had hoped it to be.

On the second to the last day of our two week itinerary, we arrived at the main train station in Milan. With a stomach full of pizza and gelato, I began to walk up the steps to catch our next train to a hotel near the airport. The beauty of the train station alone was exquisite and stunning. The city itself is the hub of all things fashion and art, and I was caught up in the moment—taking it all in. But it all changed in an instant. Immediately, my heart sank. I wasn't expecting to see what I just witnessed.

In the middle of this fashion capital, at the entrance to the beautiful station where thousands pass by each day, and out for all to see, was the most desperate and distraught young woman. Slumped down, with her back against a pillar, scantily dressed and staring into obscurity, she was sitting in her own pool of urine. Drenched as such, she was alone and hopeless.

Removed from anyone who had ever cared for her precious soul, my heart instantly began to cry for her. She was obviously strung out on drugs and in a state of great despair. She had been stripped of her dignity, and I so badly wanted her to experience the love of her Creator.

Yet, there she sat in all her brokenness for the whole world to see. My mother's heart began to pound. I was saddened, and I immediately went to prayer. It was a simple prayer, but passionate and full of faith. I prayed for a local believer to intervene in her life, at that moment and in the future. I prayed for her to experience an episodic love like never before. I prayed for angels to protect her. I prayed quick, and I prayed hard. How I wished I could speak her language and had a safe home to take her to.

With little time to spare, I proceeded to board my train. The thought of her would not leave my mind, however. What lies had she believed to get her to this point in her life? What truths about God did she doubt? Did she even believe in Him? Who and what had victimized her? What decisions had she made to get her to where she was? Even as I'm writing this, I'm thinking about her and am compelled to pray. My prayer is that, even in the midst of her brokenness, she will realize that God has never stopped loving her and is fiercely pursuing her. I will continue to pray that one day very soon, she will walk in her true identity—a redeemed and righteous daughter of the King of kings.

Biting into the lie of "did God really say" only leaves us broken and hiding in shame. All of us have stories where we've been challenged to believe lies or truth. Maybe our story isn't like the young woman in Italy, yet the challenge is common to us all. We either believe and act on lies or we believe and act on truth. When we make decisions contrary to God's standards we end up in pain and brokenness, but when we make decisions based upon God's truths we find freedom and vitality.

Let's look at spiritual brokenness and explore how it affects our souls as well as the complexities of our being. Genesis 3:7-13 speaks very clearly about true spiritual brokenness.

> Then the eyes of both of them were opened, and they realized they were naked; so they sewed fig leaves together and made coverings for themselves.
>
> Then the man and his wife heard the sound

of the Lord God as he was walking in the garden in the cool of the day, and they hid from the Lord God among the trees of the garden.

But the Lord God called to the man, "Where are you?"

He answered, "I heard you in the garden, and I was afraid because I was naked; so I hid."

And he said, "Who told you that you were naked? Have you eaten from the tree that I commanded you not to eat from?"

The man said, "The woman you put here with me—she gave me some fruit from the tree, and I ate it."

Then the Lord God said to the woman, "What is this you have done?" The woman said, "The serpent deceived me, and I ate."

In this particular passage, spiritual brokenness from God was the result of Adam and Eve being disobedient. Once it occurred, spiritual brokenness was a catalyst to hide from

God and cover their shame using fig leaves and coverings. Today, we use figurative masks and literal distractions. Spiritual brokenness is real. It's raw. It results with us asking questions like, "Will I ever feel again? Will I ever be whole again? Can I ever move on? Will I ever forget? Can I ever forgive? Can God ever love and forgive someone like me?"

The two questions God posed to Adam and Eve in the Genesis 3:7-13 passage reveal some incredible insights. They beckon us to answer and reflect upon for our own lives.

1. *Where are you?*

2. *Who told you?*

Let's unravel these a bit.

Where are you?

Just as Adam and Eve sinned and feverishly attempted to hide from God, so we follow their lead in our brokenness. We put on our own "fig leaves" hoping to cover our sin. Isn't it interesting how Adam and Eve attempted to hide from God? Isn't it interesting how we attempt to hide from God? He knows where we are. He knows everything about us.

Rather than run away from Him we must run to the ONE who can make us whole. Look how God restored the relationship with Adam and Eve. Look how He restores it with us. He asks, "Where are you?" He asks because He wants us to acknowledge our emotional and spiritual state in order to bring restoration. The question is a merciful one. He's wanting to restore us when brokenness is wanting to keep us apart.

Genesis 2:25 records that after creation Adam and Eve were both naked, but they felt no shame. It wasn't until after the Fall that they hid in shame. To them, the thought of being exposed to God was more than they could bear. They errantly believed they could cover their shame. And we are no different in our beliefs today.

Shame keeps us from returning to God. It makes us hide, causes us to forget who we are, and squelches true restoration. Reconciliation, healing and wholeness remain at bay when we avoid Him, reject Him and choose to believe that God would never want a restored relationship with us. In our brokenness, we often call evil good and good evil. We foolishly attempt to shut out the voice of God. The voice calling us today is the same voice who called out to Adam and Eve while hiding in the garden, "Where are you?"

Hiding is dark. Brokenness is painful. Isolation and loneliness are destructive. Just think, God invaded that dark space for Adam and Eve in order to release them from such pain. He knows the broken areas of our lives, and He won't stop pursuing us so that our relationship with Him is restored.

Satan will always use our weaknesses, vulnerable moments and separation to penetrate our minds with his lies. He uses crisis, the loss of control, the fear of the unknown, the fear of what others will say, the fear of being found out or the fear of missing out to deceive us. The enemy's tools are many and multifaceted. If he can keep us in our brokenness, then he can keep us from returning to God.

Humanity's tragedy throughout all dispensations has been, and will be, to dismiss God's appeal. If not remedied, brokenness perpetuates more destructiveness. Habits become stronger and mask wearing more sophisticated. Let's face it. We're all broken people and God in His love and mercy is asking us to be reconciled. He's asking all of us the question, "Where are you?"

We can be honest with God. He wants us to be. Upon Adam's confession to God that he was hiding from Him due to his nakedness, God pointedly asked, "Who told you that you were naked?"

Who told you?

Think about this. Before the Fall, Adam never realized he was naked. Nudity implies being exposed and vulnerable. Nakedness means you have something to hide, something isn't right, something is shameful, and a covering must be applied. Neither Adam nor Eve had a perception about being naked before the Fall. It was pure and natural. It was unbroken beauty. But after the Fall, Adam fully realized he was naked. How do we know this? Because God asks Adam this question. "Who told you that you were naked?"

So why did God ask Adam that question?

I believe God asked Adam to show him the author of his shame. God was asking Adam to identify the source of his shame, condemnation and brokenness. And in like fashion, God is posing these questions for us today.

Who told you that you're damaged goods? Who told you that you're unworthy? Who told you that you're unlovable? Who told you that you're broken beyond repair? Who told you that you're unforgiveable? Who told you that it's too late? Who is telling you those lies? Whose voice are you listening to? Are we listening to the voice of the enemy who is condemning us with shame and brokenness, or are we listening to the voice of our Savior, our Deliverer, our Healer?

Just as God pursued Adam, we can be certain that God is pursuing us. We may not be in the original garden, but we're living on this present earth and He's speaking directly to our soul. He's asking, "Who told you?" By implication, God is asking us to identify the source of our condemnation. We may be wanting to hide, but God is wanting us to be free. His Father's heart is yearning for us to be fully alive and fully whole, without shame and totally free.

Who has told you that your name is Shame? Who has told you that your name is Pain? Who has told you that your name is Broken? Not your God. Those aren't the names our Creator gives us. Rather, He calls us away from such names. He restores us.

Our Father is a gentleman. He gently pursues us and longs for us to come out of hiding. His love for us is greater than our poor choices and destructive decisions. Whatever the lie we fell for, God's love always counters. All He longs for is our honest answer to His questions—to answer Him with truth, accept His love and trust Him to restore. Truly, He makes *all things new!*

Reflection Questions and Action Steps:

1. We all deal differently with brokenness in our lives. God then asks, "Where are you?" When you hear this question, how have you attempted to hide the broken areas of your life?

2. Psalm 147:3 says, "He heals the brokenhearted and binds up their wounds." What broken areas of your life would you like God to heal and restore?

3. God knows everything about us. This can leave us feeling vulnerable due to the fact of being fully exposed. What are you most afraid of God seeing? What are you most afraid of others seeing? Why?

4. The question "Who told you?" is one to meditate on. What we believe about ourselves, God, our past, present and future is often spoken over our lives by many different people. We carry labels that were not created for us by God. What debilitating "names" do you feel that you, others and the enemy of your soul have spoken over you and that you're wanting freedom from?

5. Write down two to four Biblical truths that counter what the enemy of your soul has spoken

over you through other people. Make a point of speaking these truths and meditating on them throughout your day.

Chapter Three

Intervention

I'm all too familiar with breaking things. In fact, rarely does a day pass where I don't pull off some klutzy move by tripping, dropping or breaking something. You name it, I've broken it—cups, plates, bowls—the list is numerous. I'm usually left with vain attempts at trying to piece them back together. Even though I've become a master with super glue, you can still see the visible lines, flaws and weaknesses in the artifacts that were broken.

There's a Japanese artwork and philosophy called Kintsugi. It's fascinating and beautiful. So as to preserve a valuable porcelain artifact that has been chipped or broken, Japanese artists will combine a lacquer and metal dust mixture (e.g., gold, silver or platinum) to act as an adhesive and beautifier. The artist will then carefully place this adhesive mixture between the broken pieces, press the pieces back together and let set, thus creating a one-of-a-kind, stunning, ornate work of art. The visible lines of gold, silver or platinum, outlining the broken pieces, set amongst the porcelain is magnificent. Instead of attempting to hide the brokenness, the Japanese artists put their masterful touch on the broken pieces and turn the brokenness into masterpieces. The fractures are fixed, and the evidence of restoration is spectacular.

This is what God does to His children. He patiently waits until we are done trying to put our broken pieces together in our own way. He waits for us to lay our brokenness at His feet. Then, He picks up our broken pieces and gently puts us back together. His masterful hand and artistic brushstroke begin to heal and restore. And just like in Kintsugi, our brokenness then becomes the most beautiful part of us. Why? Because it has been touched by the divine hand of God, painted with His shed blood on the cross, and our renewed lives become a reflection of His glory.

In Isaiah 61:1-3 we see when God intervenes, everything changes. It says,

> The Spirit of the Sovereign Lord is on me, because the Lord has anointed me to proclaim good news to the poor. He has sent me to bind up the brokenhearted, to proclaim freedom for the captives and release from darkness for the prisoners, to proclaim the year of the Lord's favor and the day of vengeance of our God, to comfort all who

mourn, and provide for those who grieve in Zion, to bestow on them a crown of beauty instead of ashes, the oil of joy instead of mourning, and a garment of praise instead of a spirit of despair. They will be called oaks of righteousness, a planting of the Lord for the display of his splendor.

God is in the transformation business. He takes brokenness and hopelessness, flips the script, and brings beauty from ashes. He restores and renews. Notice the changes that are identified in this passage because of God's intervention and restoration.

- Good news for the poor
- Bind up the brokenhearted
- Freedom for the captives
- Release for the prisoners
- Comfort for those mourning
- Provision for those grieving
- Beauty instead of ashes
- Joy instead of mourning

- Praise instead of despair

Adam and Eve's feeble attempts to hide and avoid the wages of sin were futile. They tried to justify, remedy and cover their disobedience with their own methods. But it didn't appease, and it didn't satisfy. When their eyes were finally opened, they realized they were naked. They were vulnerable. They even made fig leaves for clothing in a vain attempt to cover their shame. But this was not God's plan, and the useless coverings failed to bring them into a restored relationship with God.

Like then, and like today, God's plan requires a sacrificial system. As death is an outcome for sin, conversely, mercy and grace through sacrifice results in restoration. The perfect, sinless sacrifice becomes the paid penalty, only because of God's great mercy and grace. The useless fig leaf garments Adam and Eve wore would need to be removed and replaced with animal skin garments. Since the "wages of sin is death" (Romans 6:23), a blood atonement was made, which was a foreshadow of Jesus Christ's blood atonement on the cross. This was given for all who are called His children. When we are restored God's way, we become clothed with Christ's righteousness.

In Genesis 3:14-15, we see God's proclamation to the enemy.

> So the Lord God said to the serpent, "Because you have done this, cursed are you above all livestock and all wild animals! You will crawl on your belly and you will eat dust all the days of your life. And I will put enmity between you and the woman, and between your offspring and hers; he will crush your head, and you will strike his heel."

Notice the deep-seated hostility between mankind and Satan back then, and notice the constant enmity there will be throughout time. The enemy will continue to nip at our heels figuratively, but through God's mercy and grace we are the declared winners.

We often give the enemy more territory, but since he's an ankle biter, and forever an ankle biter, we've been given the ability to crush his head. When he strikes with lies and temptation, our recourse is to crush his head with truth and obedience.

Through Christ paying the penalty of our sins on the cross with a crushing blow to the enemy, we have the power to crush his head. Not from our own strength and ability, but through the power of the cross. Christ alone defeats the enemy. He simply asks us to take our rightful place and position, and live in His power and freedom.

In the southern Sahara Desert of Africa, there lives a bird called the secretary bird. With long legs, a snowy white body and black tipped wings expanding to over six feet, this elegant, four-foot tall bird is quite stunning. Its legs are covered with tough scales for protection. Its small head is adorned with black plumage. Its eyes look as if war paint has been strategically applied, but the uniqueness of the bird is in how it overcomes its enemy.

The secretary bird is a powerful snake fighter. It hunts in the grasslands and preys on poisonous snakes, such as cobras and adders. When prey is found, the power of the secretary bird literally kicks in. Upon approaching the snake, the secretary bird will open its feathers wide. It then strikes mighty blows to the snake's head with an unbelievable speed of one-tenth the time it takes a human to blink their eye, and with a force that is five times its body weight. It strikes and stomps until the poisonous prey is crushed and defeated. This picture in nature offers us a strategic picture in dealing with the enemy of our soul.[1]

It's time to pull a "secretary bird" and crush our enemy's head. Jesus came to this earth and paid the price for our sin. No longer do we have to hide in shame and guilt. No longer are we sentenced to life and eternity without

Him. Through the power of the cross and our confession of faith, the enemy will be crushed.

The beautiful words of 1 John 1:9 says, "If we confess our sins, he is faithful and just and will forgive us our sins and purify us from all unrighteousness." God, through Jesus Christ and His sacrifice on the cross, freely offers forgiveness, restoration and power, so no matter what we've done, or how far we've run, His voice is calling us back to truth.

In the following chapters, we will dive deeper into God's unconditional love, forgiveness and how He makes *all things new!*

Reflection Questions and Action Steps:

1. In what ways, and in what areas of your life, does the enemy nip at your heels?

2. What have been some of your default responses when he does nip at your heels?

3. Bringing one's brokenness to God is a vulnerable process. How have you trusted or not trusted Him in the process? Give an example or two.

4. After reading how God turns brokenness into beauty, what areas of your life would you most like God to intervene and transform for you?

5. First John 1:9 says, "If we confess our sins, he is faithful and just and will forgive us our sins and purify us from all unrighteousness." Take some time and write your prayer to God confessing your sins. Thank Him for His forgiveness.

SECTION TWO
Forgiveness
Restoring Relationship with God

Chapter Four
The Reality

Imagine if you will, observing a rare glimpse into the supernatural world and you're observing it as a vision. For the very first time you're witnessing a conversation taking place in Heaven.

At first, the spiritual conversation seems to be general. Then it becomes more distinct and pronounced. Soon it becomes mind-boggling. More than you could ever imagine, intensity rises and the conversation becomes much more consequential. The more you listen, the more you realize the conversation involves you. Immediately, you discern in epic fashion that it's a conversation involving a battle for your very soul.

Zechariah 3:1-7 is depicted as that precise glimpse into a conversation in the supernatural world. There are very few occasions in Scripture where we're able to peek into such an eye-opening occurrence. At the passage onset we're introduced to the setting—the Throne Room of Heaven. Zooming in, the appearance of three characters in a judicious trial appear. They are God, Satan and Joshua, the High Priest.

> **God:** The Great I Am! The One who was, who is and who is to come! The Alpha and the Omega! The Beginning and the End! The Creator! He is all things good, all things beautiful and all things holy! He is perfect love!
>
> **Satan:** The great deceiver, liar and accuser of all humanity (Revelation 12:10).
>
> **Joshua, the High Priest:** The high priest and supreme religious leader of the day. He stands between God and the people. In the Old Testament, the high priest presented a sin offering to God to receive atonement and forgiveness for the sins of all the people.

As we peer into this passage closely, it's logical for us to place ourselves into the storied court proceeding. At the onset of the trial, we hear accusations and allegations from the Deceiver. But quickly, we're alerted to the redemption and restoration for the accused. Let's read Zechariah 3:1-7.

The Reality (Zechariah 3:1-3)
Then he showed me Joshua the high priest standing before the angel of the Lord, and Satan standing at his right side to accuse him. The Lord said to Satan, "The Lord rebuke you, Satan! The Lord, who has chosen Jerusalem, rebuke you! Is not this man a burning stick snatched from the fire?" Now Joshua was dressed in filthy clothes as he stood before the angel.

The Redemption (Zechariah 3:4-5)
The angel said to those who were standing before him, "Take off his filthy clothes." Then he said to Joshua, "See, I have taken away your sin, and I will put fine garments on you." Then I said, "Put a clean turban on his head." So they put a clean turban on his head and clothed him, while the angel of the Lord stood by.

The Restoration (Zechariah 3:6-7)
The angel of the Lord gave this charge to Joshua: "This is what the Lord Almighty says: 'If you will walk in obedience to me and

> keep my requirements, then you will govern my house and have charge of my courts, and I will give you a place among these standing here.'"

For this chapter, let's focus on Zechariah 3:1-3 — the Reality.

I don't think anything shows a better picture of humanity's story than this Zechariah passage. Here it is. You and I, humanity, dressed in filthy rags and being accused by the enemy of our souls—before a holy and righteous God—and all that is left is silence, shame and hopelessness.

But the reality is, God fiercely loves His creation. He fights for us because He loves us. He craves genuine and intimate relationship with us. He redeems and He restores.

It reminds me of a conversation I once had with a young woman.

"But you don't know what I've done! It's bad!" she expressed in anguish as she recounted her past. One story led to another. Each was filled with hurt and pain. Finally, she whispered, "I've had three abortions and countless affairs. Can God really forgive me?"

The look on her face was full of disbelief, yet I saw a glimmer of hope when I spoke God's truthful words to her. "He will absolutely forgive you, and He fiercely loves you. He's been pursuing you and calling you back. He wants to wash you, cleanse you, redeem and restore you to the person He created you to be."

With amazement and tears in her eyes, she eagerly leaned forward and said, "I want that!"

How do we respond and react when we are bombarded with the Accuser's words?

Perhaps our thoughts and emotions keep taking us to the same negative patterns of behavior. Maybe the old "movie reels" of past mistakes continue to occupy too much space in our minds, and it's affecting us greatly. It's possible we're stuck in depression, indecisiveness or feelings of powerlessness. Even more so, we might be believing the lies that we're unlovable or unforgiveable.

Thoughts of shame, condemnation and hopelessness can appear endless. Sometimes we run away. Sometimes we hide. Sometimes we blame others. Sometimes we justify our own actions. We might even lash out, behave irrationally or struggle with debilitating anger. We might retreat in pain or end all future conversation. We might become bitter, fearful and desperate.

All of it, however, is the fruit of the enemy's lies. Lies that we're doomed for a "less than life." Thoughts that situations and circumstances could never be resolved and corrected. In this false narrative, we errantly conclude that it's safer for us to wear masks and cover our brokenness, in all facets of our lives. But this is the embodiment and manifestation of the enemy's lies. The truth is, it doesn't have to end this way. Let's return to the truth. In order to do so, we must contextually understand the power of the Zechariah passage. Who is this Joshua, and why does he matter to us?

Joshua was the high priest of the Israelite nation at the time, and the one who represented the people before Almighty God. According to the Old Testament, the high priest was the one who had the unique privilege of entering the Holy of Holies once a year, on Yom Kippur, the Day of Atonement. It was his role to sprinkle the blood sacrifice on the mercy seat for the sins of himself and the Israelite people.

To further see the power of this priestly act, we must look at how the Old Testament system of forgiveness was carried out. Once a year, the high priest would remove his ornate, priestly garments and dress himself in a pure white, linen garment. He would then enter the Holy of Holies, a place where only he could enter, and proceed to offer the sacrifice.

Inside the Holy of Holies was the Ark of the Covenant, and it was the Ark (a box-like chest) that was built through God's command to Moses. It was to be a symbol that God was with His people. When Moses received the Ten Commandments (written on stone) from God, he was told to place them in the Ark. The lid of the Ark of the Covenant was known as the Mercy Seat. There were two cherubim (angels in the form of golden figurines) positioned on each end of the Ark, facing the Mercy Seat. During the once-a-year priestly offering, the high priest was commanded to enter the Holy of Holies (again, dressed in pure white linen) and sprinkle a blood sacrifice on the Mercy Seat so that the priest and all the Israelite people would receive forgiveness from God for their sins.

However, when one reads Zechariah 3:1-7, a different narrative is presented. Rather than seeing Joshua the high priest in pure white linen, we see Joshua dressed in filthy clothes—the sins of himself and his nation. We see Joshua, representing God's holy people, covered in shame and guilt. He is silent with nothing adequate to say because of his sinful condition.

And so it is with us. Satan stands before God and brings accusation after accusation. Everything he says is perceived by us to be true, and perceived to be irrefutable. But Satan is the author of lies. He creates arguments out of partial truths, as if to think that God's mercy is inadequate to atone for all of our shame and guilt. But mercy is the gift of God whereby we are not punished for our sins in the way we deserve.

Pay close attention to this next revelation. It's powerful. Remember, the Ark's Mercy Seat covering is where the atoning sacrificial blood was sprinkled by the priest. Uniquely, the Ark's Mercy Seat covering is physically located directly above the Ark's Ten Commandments. Remember, the Ten Commandments (the law for God's holy people and the law that nobody could follow perfectly this side of heaven) were the laws for which the people would be judged. Uniquely, the Ten Commandments were physically located below the Mercy Seat covering. The people would need mercy from God's judgment to cover the law they couldn't keep.

Do you see it yet?

James 2:13b states that "mercy triumphs over judgment." Amazing! Even the Ark's Mercy Seat triumphed over the judgment of not following the perfect law. Romans 3:19-25a says,

> Now we know that whatever the law says, it says to those who are under the law, so that every mouth may be silenced and the whole world held accountable to God. Therefore no one will be declared righteous in God's sight by the works of the law; rather, through the law we become conscious of our sin. But now apart from the law the righteousness of God has been made known, to which the Law and the Prophets testify. This righteousness is given through faith in Jesus Christ to all who believe. There is no difference between Jew and Gentile, for all have sinned and fall short of the glory of God, and all are justified freely by his grace through the redemption that came by Christ Jesus. God presented Christ as a sacrifice of atonement, through the shedding of his blood – to be received by faith.

It's only through God's mercy that Satan's accusations are powerless over our lives. Back to Zechariah 3:1-7. The fight was on! Satan wanted nothing but condemnation for humanity, but God silenced him. In fact, He rebuked him. I picture it as one of those discussions in which Satan's mouth was frozen shut. He had nothing more to say because of the power of the Lord's sharp rebuke. The rebuke which should have been directed to Joshua, or to us, is instead directed to Satan.

As Satan was trying to remind the people of their sin, God was reminding him of His mercy for His people. Indeed, we are His holy people. At the very moment of mercy triumphing over judgement, God put Satan in his rightful place. At the same time, God, by His mercy and love, put us in His chosen place.

God's "ace in the hole" was what He did, not what we did. There was nothing Joshua could do. Just as Joshua couldn't save himself, we too, are at the mercy of God, and He wholeheartedly, sacrificially, snatches us from the fire because He chooses us. We are His very own! We are chosen, loved and royal!

The very word, chosen, is baffling to me. A loving and merciful God has chosen us. We are chosen and He brings us to Himself. Whatever we have done in the past is not a surprise to God. He has known what our days would be like, and yet He still makes the decision to choose us and cover us with His righteousness.

In a world where there are so many hooks and conditions in people's love, it's hard to fathom such a pure love. But that's God's love. It's an unconditional love that is so deep, and a love that goes to such great lengths to redeem and to restore.

The mercy of God is like a refreshing Spring rain that pours over our tired, dirty and weary souls. It's the type of refreshing that overwhelms us with its goodness and its purity. It leaves us feeling liberated like a child running freely, and feeling more alive than ever before. This is our reality!

My friend, we can be free! Free from our past! Free from our sin! He makes *all things new!*

Reflection Questions and Action Steps:

1. How does it make you feel knowing that Satan is accusing you before the throne of God?

2. Now that you know about the mercy of God, what would you say to counter Satan's lies against you and your past?

3. God responded to Satan's accusations with a rebuke, not to Joshua (or us), but to Satan. Are you surprised by this, and how does this make you feel about God?

4. Even though our sin is fully revealed, and nothing is hidden, the Lord still chooses us. How does this influence your daily decisions?

5. Acts 3:19 says, "Repent, then, and turn to God, so that your sins may be wiped out, that times of refreshing may come from the Lord." To repent means to turn to God and turn away from those things that are against His commands. Every standard He gives us is for our freedom. When we repent, He washes us anew. Take some time in prayer and allow God's refreshing Spirit to wash you clean.

Chapter Five
The Redemption

Are we willing to go "there?" Are we willing to be completely vulnerable? Are we willing to be completely vulnerable before Him? Are we willing to accept Christ's redemptive and complete work on the cross to penetrate the secret places of our souls?

The Bible tells a story of a woman who went "there." Jesus would lead her to redemption even before she could see it and believe. That's what mercy does. It allows us to see and even believe when our lives don't deserve such gifts. Ultimately, she would find living water and refreshment for her hopeless soul. It's the story of the Samaritan woman at the well. If you can't recall the story, please allow me to recap this amazing history and take some liberties in so doing.

Like every other day, the Samaritan woman walked to the local water well to retrieve some water. Arriving at noon in the blistering heat, the Samaritan woman specifically chose this time. Why? Perhaps it was a perfect time to escape the crowds, along with their disapproving looks, underlying whispers and most hurtful of comments. She didn't need their disapproval and shame. It was no secret that she was a woman with a colorful past.

Nearing the well, she spotted a man resting on its edge. How odd, she must have thought, that a man would be at the well during the heat of day. Stranger yet, this very man began to speak to her. Did he not know that she was a Samaritan? He was a Jew. Jews let it be known that Samaritans were not worthy of them. He's surely going to let her know that she was not worthy.

But He didn't. He was a different type of Jewish man.

When we read this story in John 4:1-42, we learn of his identity. The individual was Jesus Christ, and what Jesus was about to show her during their encounter was much more than simple water retrieval for the physical body. Rather, it was about receiving living water for the soul.

Jesus asks for a drink. Her response was intended to remind Jesus that she was a second-class citizen, and not worthy to speak to a Jew. But in a moment, Jesus would turn her world upside down. Instead of heaping feelings of unworthiness on her, Jesus offers her an eternal gift.

Often, we accept "rubbish" (temporal earthly remedies) when Jesus is offering us eternal and life-changing solutions. In light of His forgiveness and renewal, we frequently dismiss His gift because we believe we're so unworthy.

Jesus tells the Samaritan woman He has living water — water that would spring up to eternal life. Her response? To ask for it so she wouldn't have to keep visiting the well day after day. Obviously, they weren't on the same page yet. He was thinking eternal, and she was thinking earthly.

But Jesus dives deeply into her heart in what appears to be an insensitive and cruel question. He draws attention to her painful past and speaks about her many husbands. Yes, He went there! Into the dark place. Into her past. Into her soul.

Why would He do this?

He wanted to set the stage for a supernatural revelation. He wanted her to have a revelation about herself, and her condition. He wanted her to know that He was God, and that He was her redeeming God. He wanted her to be aware that she was attempting to meet eternal needs with earthly means.

How many times do we respond to God the same way? In trivial fashion we dismiss His redemption. How often do we run away from our loving God because we feel so unworthy? Why do we continue to let our feelings of unworthiness keep us away from the One who redeemed us? Why do we continue to let our minds and hearts be overwhelmed by feelings of unworthiness when He has redeemed every impure act—past, present, and future?

Jesus told the Samaritan woman to go and get her husband, fully knowing she didn't have a husband. In fact, he knew she had five husbands throughout her life and the man she was currently with wasn't even her husband. The Samaritan woman was being spiritually awakened. Jesus was letting her know that the conversation wasn't about retrieving physical water, and it wasn't about finding another man. It was so much more. The Savior of the world was wanting to let her know that He was wanting to meet all of her spiritual needs. Jesus was calling her to something so real, so life-giving, so redemptive and so fulfilling. He was calling her to the source of living water and eternal life, where she would thirst no more and would be completely fulfilled. He was calling her to abundant life, this side of heaven and beyond.

Just as the Samaritan woman had tried anything and everything possible to satisfy her emotional needs, which only left her broken, alone, and hopeless, you and I often find ourselves attempting to fix our lives in the same worldly ways. And in the story, it seems as though the Samaritan woman was seeking to find reasons to preclude Jesus from giving her this living water of which He was speaking. Similarly, how often do we attempt to fulfill spiritual needs with earthly means? How often do we construct excuses and rationalize justifications to preempt God from moving in our lives?

Let's recall the Zechariah 3 passage, verses 4 and 5.

> The angel said to those who were standing before him, "Take off his filthy clothes." Then he said to Joshua, "See, I have taken away your sin, and I will put fine garments on you." Then I said, "Put a clean turban on his head." So they put a clean turban on his head and clothed him, while the angel of the Lord stood by.

In this passage, Biblical scholars seem to agree that the pronoun "I" in these verses refer to Jesus Christ. And in context, Jesus Christ our Redeemer. Jesus commanded that Joshua's filthy clothing be removed and replaced with new, fresh, linen garments. Notice how Jesus doesn't remove Himself from Joshua and his sin, but instead removed the sin from Joshua. He does the same for us.

As in the Zechariah passage, Jesus' redemption for us is initiated and facilitated by Him. It's all Him! The only part we play in the process is to invite Jesus to do His work. We can't adequately remove the stains from our lives, no matter how much we try. It's all laid bare before Jesus, even in our sophistication to cover up mistakes and hide "stains." Isn't it beautiful to know that He takes our "filthy robes" and trades them in for righteous and royal robes?

When He redeems, He no longer remembers our sin. Take a look at three scriptures that speak emphatically to this truth.

- "I, even I, am He that blots out your transgressions for My own sake, and will not remember your sins." Isaiah 43:25

- "Their sins and lawless acts I will remember no more." Hebrews 10:17

- "As far as the east is from the west, so far has He removed our transgressions from us." Psalm 103:12

The redemption picture in Zechariah reveals our good and gracious God, not a cruel and vindictive God, nor a harsh and destructive God. He could have chosen any set of attributes to define and exemplify His Deity because He's God and He's sovereign, and yet, He models attributes that are nothing less than perfect, faithful, loving and forgiving.

God doesn't owe us anything, but He chooses to be our loving Savior who fiercely pursues us. His rules and laws are intended to protect and care for us. He's not power-hungry and in need of control. He's not trying to take away our fun. Rather, He's wanting to keep us from unnecessary hurt and pain. We must admit that the consequences of rejecting and walking away from His love are overwhelmingly painful and destructive.

Perhaps you think you've done too much, and you've gone too far. The truth of the matter is that you and I can never run away from His redemptive work. There is nothing stronger, and more loving, than what Jesus Christ did on the cross. If we think there's no way God could forgive us, then in essence, we're saying that we're stronger and more powerful than God. And that's not possible! No sin, no compromise and no failure could ever have more power than the work of the cross. To suggest that God is too weak, and that His work on the cross wasn't enough, is to believe one of the Enemy's greatest lies.

The Zechariah passage paints the portrait of God putting a new, clean, white, linen garment on Joshua. But God doesn't stop there. He also puts a clean turban on his head. Why the head? Perhaps it's because the battle for our souls is won and lost in our minds. Our minds can lead us down the right or wrong path. Our minds remind us of past hurts and bitterness, brokenness and fears, even regretful memories and self-condemnation. Conversely, our minds can lead us to truth. Our minds can help us think, meditate, analyze and assess according to God's Word.

God's gracious act of putting a clean turban on Joshua's head was a symbolic act then, and it's symbolic today. It's covering our heads—our minds—with His truths. Truth is protection. His desire is for us to have the mind of Christ (Romans 12:2). We must not let the mind of the world transform us, rather, we must be transformed and renewed by His truth in our minds. What we believe about God and ourselves will determine our actions.

The Samaritan woman believed in her mind she was unclean and unworthy. We see this reflected in her many relationships. Obviously, she was trying to bring fulfillment and completion to her life outside of God's redemption and will.

What we believe about our value and our belief of what God thinks about us will always play a part in our actions. If we know our identity lies solely in the fact that we are sons and daughters of the Most High God, then we'll make decisions that honor God, ourselves and others.

As Joshua received a new turban on his head, so God has covered our heads with the mind of Christ. Instead of doubting whether God can or will redeem us, our new mind in Christ bestows an understanding that we are His image-bearers. We are His sons and daughters. We are part of His royal family. That makes us royalty!

No longer do our minds labor in shame, guilt and condemnation. Now our minds remind us that we're redeemed, restored and victorious. Second Corinthians 10:5 reminds us, "We demolish arguments and every pretension that sets itself up against the knowledge of God, and we take captive every thought to make it obedient to Christ."

As we walk securely in redemption, may our minds and hearts echo the words of our Creator in Jeremiah 31:3, "I have loved you with an everlasting love; I have drawn you with unfailing kindness." Truly, He makes *all things new!*

Reflection Questions and Action Steps:

1. In what ways can you identify with the Samaritan woman?

2. How have you tried to "clean up" your life instead of allowing Christ to do His redemptive work?

3. How have you tried to fill eternal needs with earthly things? And how has it affected your life?

4. Ponder 2 Corinthians 10:5, "We demolish arguments and every pretension that sets itself up against the knowledge of God, and we take captive every thought to make it obedient to Christ." What destructive and accusatory thoughts, beliefs and patterns of behavior do you need to take captive to Christ? What Biblical truths can you replace them with?

5. Reread the scriptures in this chapter that speak of how God completely removes our sin and chooses to remember it no more. Take some time and write a heartfelt prayer to God of how this makes you feel.

Chapter Six
The Restoration

This may be controversial, and some may find it totally unacceptable, but I have something to admit about reading fiction books. I frequently skip to the last chapter because I want to know how it ends. If it doesn't end well, I'm probably going to put the book down. I just can't help it. Maybe you feel the same.

I especially love stories of redemption and restoration. Recently, I read a remarkable story from Church history. It's one of those stories that had a beautiful ending. It's the powerful story of Photina. She was a strong and courageous woman of God who lived in the Roman Empire during the 1st century A.D. Everywhere she went, she would tell people about Jesus Christ. Without hesitation, Photina boldly proclaimed His death and resurrection. Without compromise, she would share about Jesus being the Redeemer for the world and the Hope for humanity.

Each time Photina spoke, people would commit their lives to Jesus. According to Christian tradition, she was known as being equal to the Apostles. Her tenacity and her boldness changed thousands of lives for all eternity. Who was this mighty woman? And how did she have such strength and boldness?

To set the context, Photina lived during the time of the evil Emperor Nero. In A.D. 54, Nero took the throne. He is remembered in history for not only killing his own mother, but for killing his first wife, and quite possibly his second as well. Citizens characterized Nero as half-mad as he was unpredictable and morally depraved in his actions. He killed Christians for entertainment. He issued, decreed and plotted evil willingly and liberally.

Nero condemned Christians to death by sending them to arenas filled with hungry animals where the crowds would witness their grisly demise. He would tar Christians, burn them alive and hang their bodies on poles in his gardens to use as human torches. He was a sick and ruthless tyrant. Thousands of Christians were killed because of Nero's insanity. It was in this context that the mighty woman of God, Photina, felt a personal calling by God to speak to Emperor Nero in Rome. So off she went, with her family and other Christians by her side.

Word got back to Nero that a certain woman by the name of Photina was proselytizing. He ordered his soldiers to arrest her. Ironically, before they could, she had made her way to Nero. When Nero asked her what she wanted, she told him that she had come to teach him about Jesus Christ. Photina's boldness was tenacious and unyielding.

In Photina's mind, she may have walked into the palace occupied by the most intimidating and powerful person on earth, but she was unmoved. Her power came from the God of the universe, and the royal calling she held deep within her soul came from Heaven. Committed and unafraid, Photina shared the gospel with Emperor Nero.

Church history further records that Nero rejected her message. He ordered Photina, her family and the others who accompanied her to have their hands beat repeatedly with steel rods. After three hours, the soldiers were exhausted and Nero ordered tactics to be switched. He then ordered the men in her group to be thrown into prison and he ordered Photina, along with her five sisters, into a reception hall at the Imperial Palace. All the women were seated on thrones made of gold, and before them were placed fine clothes, jewels and pure gold.

Although Nero was not at the event, he arranged for his daughter, Domnina, and her servants to persuade Photina and her sisters to renounce their faith. In a peculiar plot twist, when Photina met Domnina and her servants, she began to share about Jesus Christ and the power of the cross. Domnina, her servants and all who heard Photina's message were moved mightily. They gave their lives to Christ and were baptized.

Frustrated, Nero ordered Photina, her sisters, son and others be sentenced to death by fire. They were in a fiery furnace for seven days, and when the door of the furnace was finally opened, they walked out unharmed. They were then ordered to drink poison. Still, none of them got sick or died. For three years they were held in prison and tortured, but nothing could shake their faith. They were relentless. They continued to convert other prisoners as well as soldiers, but in the end, Nero had them all beheaded. Except for Photina. Nero had her placed in a deep, dark and dry well.

After isolation in the well and great bodily torment, Photina finally experienced Heaven releasing her from this earthly existence. She believed she had fulfilled God's purposes for her life. Soon after, God took Photina home.

Is there anything else that Church history records about Photina?

Yes. One last thing. According to Church history, Photina was the Samaritan woman at the well. Wow! What a testimony! A life so radically transformed because she had found the Living Water—Her Lord and Savior, Jesus

Christ. What a story of redemption and restoration. Jesus had become her everything, even to the point of death. [2]

Photina's past hurt and pain, shame and scandal, feelings of unworthiness and sin, had been removed. Her humdrum existence had been replaced with being fully alive. Her boldness was unequalled. Her authority unmatched. Her legacy unequivocal. Photinia was a powerful church leader and a Christian ambassador to the Roman Empire.

Although this story is not recorded in the Bible and we are relying solely on early Church history, we see Photina's story as an example of a life that has been radically transformed by Jesus Christ.

I don't know where you are in your life, but I do know that Jesus Christ is in the restoration business. He can take every last piece of our brokenness and make something even more beautiful. Romans 8:28 reminds us that God will make everything work together for our good. Even the broken things of our lives will work for our good. He restores! He repurposes! He renews!

Let's return to the Zechariah passage. Zechariah 3:6-7 states,

> The angel of the Lord gave this charge to Joshua. This is what the Lord Almighty says:

> "If you will walk in obedience to me and keep my requirements, then you will govern my house and have charge of my courts, and I will give you a place among these standing here."

Like Photina, God is restoring us to something so much more. He's inviting us to an unimaginable intimacy. He's restoring us to be positioned and anointed to walk with great authority and influence. As His royal and favored children, He desires that we walk in obedience. If we're honest, our souls crave it.

So, what is obedience?

It's completely trusting Him by making daily decisions in alignment with His Word. It's trusting His presence is always with us. It's believing He knows what's best for us and is working all things out for our good. It's knowing His timing is perfect, His peace is always available and His goodness is immeasurable. It's following His standards even if they don't make sense to us at the time.

But why is there something inside of us that screams rebellion whenever we are told that we must or should do something? What is it about us wanting to do things in our own way? Maybe you've thought, "Who is God that He should tell us how to live our lives?"

As mentioned earlier, God could have chosen to be any kind of God He wanted to be for His creation, and yet, He chose to be a kind, gracious, merciful and loving Father. Why does He have the standards that He does?

Looking into His commandments, laws and requirements, or whatever other verbiage you want to use, and looking at the natural consequences that come when we follow them or not, we can see His loving kindness for the laws He has instituted. His standards were never established to take away our fun, but they were established to keep us from unnecessary pain. Imagine a world where all of God's commands were followed. Would it be better, or would it be worse? Would there be more or less crime? Would there be stronger or weaker family units? Would there be more or less compassion for others? It's pretty obvious.

When Jesus was asked what the greatest commandment was, He replied in Matthew 22:37-40, "Love the Lord your God with all your heart and with all your soul and with all your mind. This is the first and greatest commandment. And the second is like it: Love your neighbor as yourself. All the Law and the Prophets hang on these two commandments."

Think how vastly different our world would be if everyone followed this passage of Scripture. If we loved God with all our heart, soul and mind, then we would love people as He loves them. There's a paradox in this, however. God tells us to love Him with all our heart, soul and mind, but it's not a gift to Him per se. Rather, it's a gift to us. If we love God authentically, we'll be filled with the fruit of His Spirit – love, joy, peace, patience, kindness, goodness, faithfulness, gentleness and self-control (Galatians 5:22-23). When we love ourselves first, we become overwhelmed by selfishness, hurt and pain.

Think about it like this. God could have made it where His laws and commands wouldn't benefit us at all. But He didn't. He made His laws and commands to do just that, to benefit us. In His goodness and graciousness, God gave us commandments, laws and standards. The Book of Exodus, in chapter twenty, records the Ten Commandments. Let's look at them as an example of goodness and love.

- You shall have no other gods before Me.

- You shall not make idols.

- You shall not take the name of the LORD your God in vain.

- Remember the Sabbath day, to keep it holy.

- Honor your father and your mother.

- You shall not murder.
- You shall not commit adultery.
- You shall not steal.
- You shall not bear false witness against your neighbor.
- You shall not covet.

Can you imagine if everyone in society rebelled against these standards? It would be total chaos. On the contrary, what would our world look like if everyone followed these laws? It's obvious that these standards bring safety, order and fairness to our lives. What a blessing to see the beauty of His laws. They are such sweet gifts to us. They're not heavy, nor burdensome, but in fact, quite the opposite. His laws are designed to keep pain, hopelessness and emptiness away from our lives.

The longest chapter in the entire Bible is Psalm 119. It consists of 176 verses filled with the psalmist's love and passion for God's rules, commandments and decrees. Love and affection for God's instruction is close to the psalmist's heart. The chapter records him longing to meditate on God's laws. It states that he desires to put them into practice. Let's look at a few of these verses.

"Open my eyes that I may see wonderful things in your law." (Psalm 119:18)

"I will walk about in freedom, for I have sought out your precepts. I will speak of your statutes before kings and will not be put to shame, for I delight in your commands, because I love them." (Psalm 119: 45-47)

"Oh, how I love your law! I meditate on it all day long. Your commands are always with me and make me wiser than my enemies. I have more insight than all my teachers, for I meditate on your statutes. I have more understanding than the elders, for I obey your precepts." (Psalm 119:97-100)

When my children were young, I would give them specific instructions about certain activities. I'd say, "Don't go into the road. Brush your teeth. Wear your jacket. Put your toys away. Be sure to share." Did I give them these instructions because I loved them, or because I hated them?

With each rule I gave my children, my love for them was prompting them into obedient action. I truly had their best interest in mind, then and for their future. This is the same with God. Just as my children couldn't really understand the reasons for my instructions, because they couldn't see the bigger picture, so it is with us.

Regardless of what we think or feel, our God holds fast to His standards. His laws and statutes are good for us. They bring us freedom, and if we respond with trust and obedience, we experience closeness, peace and joy.

Perhaps we feel we have gone too far. Perhaps we think we have been too rebellious or disobedient. But in it all and through it all, God is awakening us. He is not thrown by our disobedience. He wants to restore us.

Psalm 139:16-17 states, "All the days ordained for me were written in your book before one of them came to be. How precious to me are your thoughts, God!" He is the author of our lives. Perhaps we've taken the pen from Him and attempted to write our own story.

There are so many missed opportunities when we disobey God. It's freeing when we give the pen back to Him to write our personal story. He has a way of restoring lost time, lost opportunities, brokenness, abandonment, betrayal and destructive sin. He's able to complete every good work in us. Ephesians 2:8-10 promises, "For it is by grace you have been saved, through faith – and this is not from yourselves, it is a gift of God – not by works, so that no one can boast. For we are God's handiwork, created in Christ Jesus to do good works, which God prepared in advance for us to do."

There isn't any one particular sin, or combination of sins, that are more powerful than God's grace. According to Scripture, we know that sin (disobedience) brings death. This is not how God destined for us to live. John 5:21 states, "For just as the Father raises the dead and gives them life, even so the Son gives life to whom he is pleased to give it." What are the dead parts of our lives that we need God to resurrect? What purposes and plans did God write in our stories that we need to live out?

Just as with any king and his children, sons and daughters have certain privileges and authority. The Zechariah passage talks about us governing God's house and having charge of His courts. How can we govern if we don't carry out God's requirements? How can we be in charge of His house if we don't take care of it the way He would? Will we have His grace and mercy? Will we hold fast to His truth to be free, to set others free? Will we crave His righteousness, His standards, His rules and His truths?

God wants to use our stories. We are heirs of the King. We are His royal children. We are His bloodline. He wants us to walk on the restoration path—a path of obedience and a path of confidence. We are His! When a person experiences restoration at a deep, emotional level, nobody can convince them otherwise. Why? Because they know that they know, empirically, that the Lord redeems and restores.

The Lord is so good that He doesn't overlook a repentant heart, nor does He leave a repentant heart in the background. Front and center, God puts that child of the King in a place of prominence and in a place that represents Him. In these spiritual and "royal palaces," God fashions us with prestige and commissions us to go and sin no more.

Like Photina, we will shout His goodness and lead people to Him. We will silence the enemy of mankind and declare that we are the redeemed of the Lord. He says, "Go, and sin no more!" No more squalor. No more poverty. No more shame. We are free!

He calls us, "Chosen, Beloved, Son and Daughter." In 1 Peter 2:9 we are reminded, "But you are a chosen people, a royal priesthood, a holy nation, God's special possession, that you may declare the praises of him who called you out of darkness into his wonderful light." When we believe this, we walk differently, talk differently and live differently. We see our journey on this earth through the lens of eternity, and the things of this world no longer entice us. Instead, our hearts yearn to abide in Him.

Just as Joshua was offered a place of governorship in the house of the Lord and exhorted to walk in obedience, so we too are offered the same gift. We have not sinned too much, or traversed too far, beyond the reach of our loving Heavenly Father. He has never stopped pursuing us.

We're restored. Let's take our royal position and walk into our royal destiny. He makes *all things new!*

*Perhaps you've read the first half of this book and have never made a decision to accept Jesus Christ as your Lord and Savior. If so, I encourage you to jump to the back of the book right now and read the section entitled, "The Most Important Decision."

In it, you will discover the greatest gift that has ever been offered to you. If accepted, you won't be the same. And just like I mentioned at the beginning of this chapter of how I read the last chapter first, I want you to jump to the end of this book – because then I will know your story will have a great ending.

Reflection Questions and Action Steps:

1. Describe how obeying God's laws bring freedom.

2. What areas of your life do you need to turn over to God in order to walk in obedience?

3. Do you truly believe that God has a beautiful story written for your life? Why or why not? What are some steps you can take to live out God's story for your life?

4. First Peter 2:9 states, "But you are a chosen people, a royal priesthood, a holy nation, God's special possession, that you may declare the praises of him who called you out of darkness into his wonderful light." How does this encourage and empower you?

5. As you commit to walking His royal plan for your life, write a prayer of thankfulness to God. You might focus on relishing in the truth that He will never stop loving you. Let this prayer be a reminder of the restoration He is doing in you.

SECTION THREE
Forgiveness
Restoring Relationship with Others

Chapter Seven
Christ's Model for Forgiveness

For Sabina, pleasure and amusement were incessant. Partying was her passion. Indulgent and questionable living described her behavior, but it was frowned upon by her family—Orthodox Jews in the Austro-Hungarian Empire.

Sabina lived in the 1900s. She lived through the horrors of Germany's Hitler, and survived the Communist takeover by the Russians. Her life was controlled, difficult and burdensome. Partying seemed to free her from the tyranny.

Sabina would soon marry Richard, and together they established a family. But her partying continued. They established a home in Bucharest, Romania, but after some time, Richard became tragically struck with sickness. Tuberculosis threatened his life, but it was through this experience that Richard found Jesus Christ to be his personal Lord and Savior.

Richard had come to realize that the Jesus Christ of the New Testament wasn't the anti-Jewish cult figure he once thought Christianity to be. When God healed Richard of tuberculosis, Sabina began to question her own life, faith and purpose. She too came to realize the gravity of her sinful life and accepted Jesus Christ as her Lord and Savior. It would be this very grace and forgiveness Sabina experienced from Jesus that would lead her to offer the same love and forgiveness to others who persecuted her, Richard, and those whom she loved greatly.

As Communism took over Romania in 1945, following the death of Hitler, Richard and Sabina had become powerful spiritual leaders to those around them. Their boldness and faith were unmatched. In a time of atheism and tyranny, their determination to share the love of Jesus with their fellow countrymen was relentless. It would eventually land them in prison, however.

It was a dangerous time to be a Christian. The church had no choice but to meet in secret. Christians often turned on one another by telling authorities about such secret meetings. This caused Sabina to feel anger and bitterness grow in her heart towards disloyal Christians. She couldn't fathom such betrayal.

On a particular occasion, while contemplating the betrayal, Sabina's eyes landed on a picture of Jesus on the cross.

His words immediately sprung to her mind, "Father, forgive them, for they do not know what they are doing" (Luke 23:34). At this, her heart suddenly changed toward her betrayers. She realized she needed to forgive them and offer Christ's unconditional love to them, just as He had for her. This sudden realization literally changed her life and ministry. [3]

One day, Richard met a man whom he had never met before. The man's name was Borila. Borila happened to be an old friend of Richard and Sabina's landlord. After their introductions, the three men spoke at great length. During their conversation, Borila boasted about his past. He bragged about killing hundreds of Jews, specifically in the area of Transmistria. Unbeknownst to Borila, this was the area where Sabina's parents, brother, three sisters and other relatives had been taken to lose their lives in a concentration camp.

As Borila boasted, Richard thought to himself that the very man he was talking to could quite possibly be the killer of Sabina's family. But Richard didn't say anything. Borila had yet to meet Sabina as she was asleep in their downstairs flat, but the two men continued to talk about everything under the sun. They shared their passions and interests. They shared their lives. Borila expressed his love for Ukrainian music and Richard expressed his love for the piano.

The talk soon led to Richard inviting Borila to his personal flat so that he could play Borila some Ukrainian music on his piano. Elated at the opportunity, Borila joined him.

After Richard played for a while, and the two enjoyed good fellowship, Richard felt prompted to have a heart-to-heart conversation with Borila about the Lord.

Richard wanted to tell him about God's love. But before he shared the gospel, Richard reminded Borila about what he had bragged about earlier in the evening—about his personal involvement in the killing of many Jewish people. Sabina was sleeping in the next room and unaware of the conversation as Richard spoke.

Richard divulged to Borila that Sabina's family had been killed in Transmistria. There was a guarded and wary look in Borila's eyes when he heard this information, but Richard proceeded. Richard then suggested that Borila might have been the very person who was responsible for killing Sabina's family members. At that very instance, Borila shot up from his seat. Anger and anxiety manifested, but Richard, calm and collected, kindly raised his hand and gently suggested, "Let's try an experiment."

Borila was bewildered. Richard continued. "I shall wake my wife and tell her who you are and what you've done. But before you come to a conclusion, I will tell you what will happen. When my wife learns of it, she will not speak one word of reproach to you. She'll embrace you as if you were her brother. She'll bring you supper and the best things she has in the house. Remember, if Sabina, who is a sinner like us all can forgive you, and love like this, imagine how Jesus, who is perfect love, can forgive and love you. Only turn to Him, and everything you've done will be forgiven!"

Borila was overwhelmed by Richard's words and testimony. He was filled with grief and sorrow. Borila fell to his knees, sobbed and pleaded for the forgiveness of God. Richard then led Borila in a time of repentance and prayer, and both men knew that God had touched Borila. Richard knew he needed to do one more thing. He went to his sleeping wife and said, "Sabina, there's a man here whom you must meet. We believe he has murdered your family, but he has repented, and now he is our brother."

Richard was so confident in the depth of God's love living through his wife Sabina that he knew exactly what her response would be to Borila. And just like he said, Sabina greeted Borila with love and overwhelmed him with a huge hug, welcoming him into God's family. They all began to cry and embrace as God's forgiveness and healing touch washed over them. And true to Richard's premonition, Sabina went and prepared Borila food. [4]

This powerful testimony of mercy, grace and forgiveness is nothing short of supernatural. It's very difficult to forgive those who have harmed us or those who have harmed the ones we love. Just the mention of forgiving "that person" may put knots in our belly, stir us to anger or bring us to tears. To forgive "that person" often feels like letting them off the hook when their actions don't deserve such mercy. No doubt, forgiving an offense is easier said than done.

To truly forgive others, one must begin with a deep dive into understanding God's forgiveness for what we've done to Him. Without God extending His forgiveness to us, our ability to forgive would be impossible.

We've all forged unique experiences and have lived different stories. Some of us have experienced deep pain and loss at levels others find impossible to understand. Some stories are so egregious and horrendous that to forgive implies being irrational. But if we're honest, we should have a difficult time not forgiving another, in light of what Jesus has done for us.

Over the years, I've personally observed one of the greatest keys for unlocking our God-given potential is forgiveness.

It's the very key that brings emotional, relational and spiritual freedom. Conversely, I've witnessed people taking unforgiveness to their death bed, ending in unnecessary bitterness and pain when they could have freed themselves and others.

When we gaze upon Him with a heart of gratefulness for the forgiveness and restoration He so freely offered us, we begin to understand. It's truly divine. Our Savior's example is the perfect standard.

It's imperative we understand the meaning of the words grace and mercy so we can truly forgive others. Grace is receiving a gift we don't deserve, and mercy is not receiving what we do deserve. For example, grace is receiving the gift of Heaven (which we don't deserve) and mercy is not receiving the punishment of Hell (which we do deserve). Our sin deserved eternal separation and death from God, but Jesus forgave us and freed us from our debt, bestowing upon us eternal life. That's mercy and grace!

As we move forward and work through the process of forgiving others, it's important to see how Christ modeled this for us. The weight of carrying unforgiveness towards others affects every area of our lives. It's a weight we were never meant to carry, and Jesus graciously gave us a pattern to follow. Jesus says in Matthew 11:28-30, "Come to me, all you who are weary and burdened, and I will give you rest. Take my yoke upon you and learn from me, for I am gentle and humble in heart, and you will find rest for your souls. For my yoke is easy and my burden is light."

Jesus, the ultimate teacher, knows the weight of unforgiveness is crushing to the human soul. It was never the pattern set before us. Instead, He urges us to trust Him as a gentle and loving teacher, to lay our burdens at the foot of the cross. In this, we will find rest.

Eugene Peterson paraphrased this passage beautifully in the Message Bible. "Are you tired? Worn out? Burned out on religion? Come to me. Get away with me and you'll recover your life. I'll show you how to take a real rest. Walk with me and work with me – watch how I do it. Learn the unforced rhythms of grace. I won't lay anything heavy or ill-fitting on you. Keep company with me and you'll learn to live freely and light."

If we carry hurt, pain and unforgiveness, we become bogged down, weary, bitter, tired, frustrated and angry. Instead, Jesus says to learn from Him, to keep company with Him, and then our souls will be at rest. What He asks us to carry is light compared to the heavy burden of unforgiveness.

Let's be honest. It might be a little difficult to read, let alone obey, but Jesus is speaking this to relieve us of our burdens. Matthew 6:14-15 states, "For if you forgive other people when they sin against you, your Heavenly Father will also forgive you. But if you do not forgive others their sins, your Father will not forgive your sins."

This might sound harsh, unfair and unattainable at first glance, but when we truly grasp the measure of His grace and mercy, then this becomes possible, desirable and attainable. If Jesus did not extend His forgiveness to us and left us in our own depravity, we would be eternally separated. It's His love flowing into us, and then out of us, that gives us the desire, ability and strength to forgive others.

Let's attempt to put ourselves in God's "shoes" for a moment. The Scriptures paint a picture of Jesus walking amongst His creation whom He masterfully created and fashioned from His image. A loving Savior who breathed His very breath into mankind, gave humanity everything they needed for sustenance, sacrificed everything for them, even His life, only to be rejected, mocked and crucified. Indeed, God has unjustly experienced ultimate rejection and betrayal from His creation.

Throughout Jesus' earthly ministry He was hit with roadblocks by the Pharisees and Sadducees—the religious leaders who should have been closest to Him. Instead of honoring Him, they mocked, ridiculed and lied about Him.

He went from town to town offering healing, hope and forgiveness, and yet many, even His own family, doubted and scoffed at Him.

Being the King of kings, Jesus didn't evoke His rightful and royal authority. Even His birth was the humblest of circumstances. He lived on this earth as a servant. He loved like no other. He chose to endure the most painful, humiliating death because He didn't want to spend eternity without us. How can one even begin to comprehend the love that held Him on the cross during the crucifixion?

He was beat, whipped, spit on and nailed to the cross by the same hands that He lovingly created. He listened to His creation mock and hurl insults with the very mouths He formed. He looked upon the soldiers inflicting torture and causing Him inexplicable physical pain by the same bodies He shaped. And, in all the jeering and injustice, we read in Luke 23:34 that He lovingly prayed, "Father, forgive them, for they do not know what they are doing." Humanity didn't keep Jesus on the cross. His love for them did.

How could He extend mercy, grace and forgiveness to them—to us? He who lived a perfect, sinless life and never harmed a soul, would be misunderstood, mistreated, falsely accused, abased, ridiculed and betrayed, and yet He would lovingly forgive with an unconditional, deep, transcendent love. It's His great love that compels Him to forgive.

And He asks us to forgive others. Too difficult? Impossible? Unfair?

We may fail to realize, however, that when He asks us to forgive others, it really is about Him offering a gift to us. If we compare two people who have been hurt in similar fashion, and one chooses forgiveness and the other doesn't, the one who chooses forgiveness will most likely walk in unfathomable freedom. Comparatively, the one who does not offer forgiveness will carry bitterness, anger and resentment like a poison that causes a slow death to themselves and their relationships. Forgiveness allows for peace and joy. Forgiveness makes us stronger, more beautiful, more joyful and more compassionate.

When our heavenly Father tells us to forgive as He forgave, it empowers us in two major ways. First, it allows us to see the fullness of His grace, mercy and redemption that is freely bestowed upon us. Second, it offers us an inexplicable freedom. The offender can no longer control our minds and hearts when we offer them forgiveness. In the greatest sense of empowerment, it's a release, freedom and strength.

Ephesians 5:1-2 states, "Follow God's example, therefore, as dearly loved children and walk in the way of love, just as Christ loved us and gave himself up for us as a fragrant offering and sacrifice to God." Through the act of forgiving and offering of mercy and grace to our offender, we are building a bridge of freedom for them to mightily experience God's love and truth—as are we.

But what if, in the very depths of our hearts, we don't want those who have offended or hurt us to be forgiven and walk in freedom? What if we want them to suffer? This is where we must go back to the cross and release them knowing that our perfect and holy God forgave us even when we didn't deserve it.

Except by His forgiveness, there is nothing we can do to walk in right standing with a holy God. We are sinful in light of His perfection. When we realize we're on the same playing field as those who so deeply hurt us, and our sin is as great as theirs, then we have the ability to move in forgiveness. We may think our offending party did so much worse than we ever did, but who are we to set the boundary line of what is and isn't forgivable? Romans 3:23-24 states, "For all have sinned and fall short of the glory of God, and all are justified freely by his grace through the redemption that came by Christ Jesus."

The more we believe and operate in knowing God, His character, His nature, His holiness and His forgiveness, the more willing we are to offer forgiveness to others. When we experience God for who He really is, we find great joy in forgiving because we are loving the way we have been loved. It's as if we see ourselves through our offender's sin, and thus, the need for our loving Savior's forgiveness. Colossians 3:13 encourages us. "Bear with each other and forgive one another if any of you has a grievance against someone. Forgive as the Lord forgave you."

Forgiving others is laying down our rights—the right for vindication, for an apology, for getting even. Forgiving is an act of obedience, and it's an act that reveals our gratefulness to God. Offering forgiveness to others is our love response to Him. Our gift back to God is our choice to love and forgive others as this reveals our true understanding of the depth of God's love, mercy, grace and forgiveness to us.

Ephesians 4:29-32 states, "Do not let any unwholesome talk come out of our mouths, but only what is helpful for building others up according to their needs, that it may benefit those who listen. And do not grieve the Holy Spirit of God, with whom you were sealed for the day of redemption. Get rid of all bitterness, rage and anger, brawling and slander, along with every form of malice. Be kind and compassionate to one another, forgiving each other, just as in Christ God forgave you."

If this chapter has seemed a bit tough to digest, let's pause and reflect on the incredible love our Savior has for us. Truly, He will walk the journey of forgiveness with us. It's His love for us that gives us the strength to forgive others. Remember, we can trust Him. He is gentle and thoughtful. In the next chapter we will dive deeper into the why and how of forgiving others. Remember, He makes *all things new!*

Reflection Questions and Action Steps:

1. Do you find it hard to forgive someone in your life? Why or why not?

2. What are the first things that come to mind when you read the following passage in Matthew 6:14-15? "For if you forgive other people when they sin against you, your Heavenly Father will also forgive you. But if you do not forgive others their sins, your Father will not forgive your sins."

3. How does receiving God's grace and mercy empower you to forgive others?

4. What are the benefits in forgiving others?

5. How does carrying unforgiveness hurt you? How does it affect your relationships with others?

Chapter Eight
Forgiving Others

The betrayal! The dishonor! The pain!

It wouldn't hurt so deeply if the person didn't mean so much to us, but human connection runs deep. Offenses from others hurt and divide in unimaginable ways. There's the broken relationship that left us in pieces and the painful experience that ripped our heart out. It's true, relationships can be some of our greatest joys, but broken relationships are often our most troubling sorrows.

"I trusted them. I was vulnerable. I let them into my world and just as soon as they garnered my trust and confidence, they betrayed me. How could I have let my guard down? Why didn't I see this coming? Why are they now blaming me? Why are they abandoning me? I'm wounded." Such thoughts appear to be endless.

Forgive them? Inconceivable! Forget? Impossible!

Just being human, you've experienced the offense of others at some level. It's part of life. We live in a fallen world.

Maybe you've experienced the offense of others in the form of abandonment, divorce, physical, emotional or sexual abuse, or perhaps you've experienced sophisticated manipulation at the highest level with infidelity. Perhaps you were lied to, or maybe you were lied about. No matter the circumstance, no matter the uniqueness of the story, the same seed has been planted. Will it take root?

The toxic root of bitterness can spread wide, grow deep, fortify and multiply. Each time we replay and review our painful hurts and betrayals, even rehearse our silent or audible responses, roots of bitterness have the potential to entrench our hearts. And if they're never addressed, emotional and spiritual paralysis will set in.

Forgiving others is one of the most difficult tasks set before us. How do we even begin to forgive those who have so grievously offended us? And why should we? Why should we even forgive others when they haven't repented of their wrongdoing and sought reconciliation?

The result of living in a fallen world is brokenness. Broken people beget broken people. Hurt people hurt people, and the consequences proliferate great pain and subsequent offense. Just as Satan's goal is to invite all of humanity into his brokenness, humanity's default is to do the same to each other.

The Bible says it best in James 4:1-3. "What causes fights and quarrels among you? Don't they come from your desires that battle within you? You desire but do not have, so you kill. You covet but you cannot get what you want, so you quarrel and fight. You do not have because you do not ask God. When you ask, you do not receive, because you ask with wrong motives, that you may spend what you get on your pleasures."

Selfishness causes humanity to hurt each other for many reasons. The hurt generally stems from one or more of these five categories.

1. Personal Past Pain and Battles

2. Wrong Perceptions

3. Pride

4. Physical Weaknesses

5. Evil Intentions

Let's dive into each of these categories in an attempt to bring some understanding of the offenses that have targeted us personally.

Personal Past Pain and Battles

In everyone's personal story, vulnerable flaws, dysfunction and intimate details are often masked by pretentious outward behavior. Hidden pain, unresolved sin, internal struggle, deep grief, chaos and confusion all become masked. To some degree or another, all of us can and will carry any one of these around at some point in our journey on earth.

My husband, Scott, served in education for years, first as a teacher and then as a principal. Successfully working with the most at-risk individuals, I called him the "teen whisperer" due to his uncanny ability to discern the hearts of students.

It's not uncommon for educators to complain about student disrespect and lack of engagement. It's also not uncommon for frustrated and impatient educators to trigger students. In so doing, student misbehavior manifests even greater. But through it all, Scott would encourage educators around him to make deposits into their students' lives so as to connect with them. He also encouraged educators to know their students' personal stories. He has always said, "Find out what their story is and there you will find the why of their behavior."

Knowing that a student's lack of engagement could stem from a multiple of reasons, like trying to manage crisis, pain or struggle, is key to discerning and understanding. The disconnect felt in the classroom could be from a family dispute the night before. It could be a feeling of insecurity related to not knowing content matter. It could be feeling "stupid." It could be something as simple as disapproving looks or negative words from others, maybe even from the teacher. But through it all, Scott would say, "Every student has a story. We must learn it. We must walk a mile in their shoes to understand them." Essentially, Scott was saying learning their story brings understanding as to their motive.

In the same way an educator seeks to know their students' stories, we need to understand how injustices done to us and offenses directed toward us often come from the offender's own past personal pain and former battles. In no way does it excuse their behavior toward us, but it does give us an understanding as to the why. There's always a story behind the offender offending.

When we judge the offender without attempting to understand their story, we base the judgement on our own standards of acceptability. In many cases, it's quite possible the person who inflicted hurt against us is an individual who has yet to work through a prior crisis or incident. They might be needing to forgive somebody else.

Since hurt people hurt others, the offender's actions are often learned behavior. These actions involve lashing out, destructive words, demonizing, victimizing, manipulating, condescending words, aggressive words or actions, and any other negativity that has been gleaned from their past.

The cycle will always continue to repeat itself from person to person, family to family, until there is an individual who chooses to work through their shortcomings, develop positive strategies to overcome hurting others, forgive and release the strongholds of bitterness and pain. When we choose to not personalize every offense, realizing the other person's behavior could be a manifestation of their own internal struggles, we free ourselves from carrying the weight of anger and bitterness.

Wrong Perceptions

Perception involves noticing or understanding things using our senses. When dealing with understanding human behavior, the challenge lies in whether we perceive intentions correctly or incorrectly. Our default is to perceive another's actions and intentions based upon our own life experiences, worldview and personality. Therein lies the challenge.

How can we adjust? How can we look through the lens of another? How can we avoid creating our own version of perceived truth to address conflict and misunderstanding?

Perhaps an individual was raised in a negative and pessimistic home environment. They would then look at comments, actions and perceived intentions through this lens of negativity. By default, they would assume the worst of intentions in people rather than seeking to understand that the other person might not be operating with negative intentions as are being perceived.

Perhaps a person grew up in a controlling household and they see everything someone does as trying to control them. By default, that individual is sensitive to the appearance of control and may impulsively lash out with sudden and hurtful comments to avoid perceived control—leaving the other person confused and anxious.

Categorizing people into defined groups and expecting their behavior to be a specific pattern without allowing their true self and intentions to emerge minimizes them as a person. In a sense, it reduces their identity and truest humanity. This is why we must seek to understand people and ascertain the most empirical perception as possible.

Inaccurate perceptions will always lead to negative outcomes—some minutely negative and others destructively harmful. Most of us have experienced a moment when we've communicated to an individual or a group, and said something that was taken the wrong way. Their perception of what we said wasn't what we intended. Feelings were hurt. In some cases, relationships were broken. It makes one wonder how many of our broken friendships and relationships have come from simply having the wrong perception of another person's intentions.

Accurate perception and proper discernment are some of the greatest gifts we can possess. To sense what an individual is feeling or trying to say can bring connection. Responding compassionately and appropriately follow when we study others and learn to ask detailed and open-ended questions, observe body language and expression, as well as tone and context. In life, sometimes we get it right and sometimes we get it wrong, but in all of it, growth will take place and better discernment will ensue.

Moving forward, it's imperative we slow down and find the truth in all situations. Our Creator intends for us to have proper discernment, and His Holy Spirit is faithful to help us. Attempting to objectively seek truth in all actions and expressions directed toward us will go a long way in releasing offense in our hearts. It's also important to remember to evaluate whether or not the offense we feel from another person was truly their intention, and not just our perception.

Pride

Nothing beneficial comes from pride. The Bible says that pride comes before a fall. Some of the greatest offenses have been caused because of it. In the first book of Samuel, chapters 9-31, we learn of a national leader's pride and the subsequent consequences.

You might know the story. Young Saul, an Israelite from the tribe of Benjamin, would become the first king of the nation of Israel. He stood at least a head taller than everyone else. His handsome features caused heads to turn. Young, strong and raised by an unassuming family, Saul couldn't help but stand out from the crowd.

Initially, Saul was humble. The very thought of him being a king for his nation scared him. In fact, if you read the story, you'll find that he was hiding while the authorities were pronouncing him as king. Yet, the Lord molded him and he became a powerful leader.

As the years progressed, Saul's leadership became less focused on God and more on himself. He began to compromise. Pride crept in. Saul would seek the applause of men rather than God. In 1 Samuel 15, we find that Saul had just returned from a battle against the Amalekites, and in this battle, Saul had disobeyed God's battle instructions. As the prophet Samuel sought to confront Saul, he learned Saul had gone off to Carmel to set up a monument to honor himself. Indeed, pride had found its way into Saul's heart.

When the prophet Samuel confronted Saul and told him that he would be replaced as king because of his sin, Saul was more concerned about how he would look in front of the people rather than seeking restoration with God. Saul said to Samuel in 1 Samuel 15:30a, "I have sinned. But please honor me before the elders of my people and before Israel." Obviously, pride had consumed Saul. Appearing successful in his countrymen's eyes was what led to his downfall.

As Saul's kingdom was being taken from him, the new upcoming king, the young shepherd boy, David, was anointed. David would have to wait for God's perfect timing to rule the Israelite nation, and while in the process he would serve as a faithful court aide to King Saul.

Extreme loyalty described David's service to King Saul, but Saul was jealous of David. On several occasions, King Saul attempted to kill David. Pride, jealousy and fear reigned in Saul's heart as he perceived David to be a threat. Amidst all the offenses and injustices, David never once sought to take revenge on Saul. He was above reproach. He trusted God's timing and vindication. Could this be why the Bible states that David was a man after God's own heart?

Saul's story is really humanity's story. Pride creeps into our hearts and gives rise to thoughts of jealousy, fear, inferiority and so much more. It grows, spreads and weakens. It refuses to apologize. It builds arrogance. It elevates self. It lusts. It squashes compassion. It removes God.

As Saul threw spears at David, so our pride causes us to throw relational spears by dethroning others and making them look inadequate or inferior, irrelevant or insignificant. Experiencing the spears from others' pride is an offense we've all experienced. Pride is always traced to being self-focused and self-absorbed.

The anecdote to pride is found in Philippians 2:5-7. "In your relationships with one another, have the same mindset as Christ Jesus: Who, being in very nature God, did not consider equality with God something to be used to his own advantage; rather, he made himself nothing by taking the very nature of a servant, being made in human likeness.

And being found in appearance as a man, he humbled himself by becoming obedient to death, even death on a cross."

Physical Weaknesses

We all are predisposed to physical weakness in our bodies because of living in a fallen world. One of the most overlooked reasons why people hurt others is because of the breakdown of their physical bodies. We are all scientific labs. At times, people operate with negative actions when their self-systems are not harmonious.

Think back to the times in your life when you've lacked sleep or were hungry. How about sickness, injury, stress or unstable blood sugar? Human responses to any of these can be frustration, negativity, anger or impatience. It's not uncommon to take out on others what we're feeling physically. Unfortunately, we've all received an offense, or have been the offender, because of these types of tendencies and physical weaknesses.

When we find ourselves on the receiving end of someone's hurtful words or actions, we must be aware of how they're feeling physically. Are they running on empty? Have they missed necessary sleep? Have they skipped a meal? Have they eaten too much sugar or ingested too much caffeine?

Are they sick? Have they recently been injured? Do they have a chronic, painful disease? Are they under a lot of stress?

Let's dig deeper into these.

Sleep: Sleep is a leading contributor to emotional stability. As an adult, we should have seven or more hours of sleep each night. When lacking sleep our bodies go into survival mode. We take things more personal. We get triggered more easily. We snap at people. Ordinary things become more pronounced and bothersome. We say things we wouldn't normally say. And the list goes on. Sleep deprived individuals often offend or cause pain to others, and may not even realize the relational damage that is being caused.

Food: Our bodies are chemical laboratories and what we eat, or don't eat, affects our entire wellbeing. Excessive sugar in our diets, caused from too many refined sugars or too many carbohydrates, can cause erratic behavior and mood swings. Even not having enough protein can do the same. Chemical imbalances are real because of food and nutrition issues. Even chemicals in our foods, or food allergies, can greatly affect a person's behavior and wellbeing.

Sickness and Injuries: Feeling sick, dealing with a temporary or chronic illness, disease or pain, can affect people.

When their bodies are hurting, almost everything bothers them. They have used most of their energy to deal with their physical pain. This leaves them drained and disadvantaged in dealing with their emotional wellbeing. Many who are in a close relationship with someone experiencing physical sickness will bear the brunt of the other's painful manifestations.

Stress: We all experience stress. It comes from work, home, busy schedules, leadership roles, responsibilities, demanding relationships and so much more. People handle stress differently. Some let it out and others keep it in. Being aware of stress, in others and ourselves, can certainly help us navigate positive courses of action.

Evil Intentions

Jeremiah 17:9 states, "The heart is deceitful above all things and beyond cure. Who can understand it?"

Throughout history, the human heart has unleashed the darkest of depravity on this world. Ruthless tyrants, evil dictators and dark rulers in the likes of Hitler, Stalin and Pol Pot, have hurt and destroyed in ways that are too evil to write about. Millions upon millions of innocent lives have been destroyed and murdered because of them.

Luke 6:45 says, "A good man brings good things out of the good stored up in his heart, and an evil man brings evil things out of the evil stored up in his heart. For the mouth speaks what the heart is full of."

How do we even begin to understand vile, dark and pure evil? How does one fully understand darkest depravity imposed on innocent individuals? How can we understand rape, molestation, murder, slavery, domestic violence, child abuse and so much more? To be honest, we really can't, but the Bible categorizes it as evil. Evil hearts perpetuate evil atrocities.

For those who have been victims of abuse, forgiveness can seem overwhelmingly impossible. These feelings and emotions are understandable, but in spite of the pain we might be living with because of past injustices done against us, God has a way for us to move forward. He has given us every eternal resource in heaven in order to release the strongholds that have been placed in and over our lives. Stay with me, for the spiritual keys to unlocking doors we thought were forever closed are about to be delivered. Walking in forgiveness and freedom are quite possibly just steps away.

Separating the Offense from the Offender

Perhaps we've allowed our past pain and unforgiveness to become the major focus of our lives. In a sense, it has become our god. It has affected our allegiance, our beliefs and our unwillingness to surrender to God. Let's say it this way. When we've propped up the idol of pain or bitterness, and God no longer takes first place, then we cease to feel and experience His peace and presence. At this point, the destructive fire—a fire that consumes how we think, how we feel and how we view our yesterday, today and tomorrow—is fully all-consuming.

When pain becomes our god, it will make us into its very own image. Instead of bearing the image of God, we bear the image of pain. In doing so, we become bound to it telling us who we are, what decisions we must make and how we must operate. It affects how we view ourselves and how we interact with others.

The hurt against us must not turn us into a person we were never created to be—a person filled with anger, bitterness, brokenness or sadness. Yet, forgiveness releases the power of the offender over our lives and allows us to become what God intended us to be—a soul operating with peace, power and purpose.

When we forgive someone who has deeply hurt us, we're not saying what they did to us was right. We're not condoning their action against us, nor are we justifying their offense. Instead, we forgive them, so we no longer carry the burden and the power of their evil against us. God himself tells us that He will carry the burden.

Let's look at separating the offense from the offender through the lens of a spiritual paradigm – through spiritual eyes, and not through natural eyes. It's a spiritual realm that is quite revealing to the ploys of the enemy. Ephesians 6:12 states, "For our struggle is not against flesh and blood, but against the rulers, against the authorities, against the powers of this dark world and against the spiritual forces of evil in the heavenly realms."

If we're to assume there's a spiritual battle being waged, then we have to conclude that the enemy is real and his goal is destruction. This means the enemy carries out his destructive desires through the darkness of human hearts. He uses any vice, a plethora of manipulations, evil inclinations and chaotic agendas to bind up and destroy. He uses humanity's selfishness, the desire for power, pride, envy, greed, deceit and the list goes on, to be the instruments of his dark world. He is so sly and so tricky.

From a spiritual lens, the enemy is constantly at work with evil objectives and purposes. John 10:10a states, "The thief comes only to steal and kill and destroy." Just knowing this allows us to evaluate the subtle as well as the obvious evil at work. First Peter 5:8-9a states, "Be alert and of sober mind. Your enemy the devil prowls around like a roaring lion looking for someone to devour. Resist him, standing firm in the faith."

Through the lens of this scripture, all of us are susceptible to the ploys and tactics of the enemy. He is sly, scheming and deceitful. All of us need to assess how the enemy is trying to destroy us through any particular evil that has come against us. Above all, the enemy desires that we never separate the offense from the offender. If we accept his manipulation, then we will always see the other person through natural eyes (our flesh). He wants us to react to offense in the flesh, rather than in the Spirit.

Freedom comes when we begin to separate the offense from the offender. When we see our offender as created by God, in a spiritual battle with the enemy who is trying to sabotage their life and take their soul, we can begin to see them more than just a person who offended us. We begin to see them through a spiritual lens—as broken vessels, just as we are, in need of a loving Savior.

I know some have experienced evil that is so egregious and wicked, even blasphemous. For many, such heinous and unthinkable acts of evil have victimized so destructively that the natural human mind perceives forgiveness to be inconceivable. How can one forgive such evil acts and evil perpetrators? This may seem impossible. And honestly, it is impossible in the natural.

However, through God's supernatural power, we are given the strength to forgive – even the most evil and vile. God's great love enables us to forgive so that we may be free from the hurt, anger and bitterness. Forgiveness is an act of faith. It doesn't mean that we condone, but it means that we release the power of the evil against us. As free moral agents, we can choose to let unforgiveness reign in our hearts or we can choose to take a step of faith and forgive. In so doing, we release ourselves from the strongholds that have come against us.

Because of God's great love for us, He wants us free. Forgiveness is a release. It's freedom. It empowers us to be released from the destructive evil that has come against us. The ability to forgive, even in the most horrible of experiences, is a supernatural act and strength that comes from the Holy Spirit. He will vindicate us. All we must do is act in faith. It's truly supernatural.

Only God is perfect and holy. All of us have sin that is equally egregious in light of a pure and righteous God. If not for Jesus offering his mercy and grace, and paying the penalty for our sins, all of us would be doomed to live forever in the consequences of our mistakes. Humanity tends to create their own evaluative tool to assess what is more right and what is more wrong, but in light of holiness and perfection, all sin is wrong. All humanity has fallen short of the glory and perfection of God.

Wrong doing (sin) always demands judgment, yet Jesus will not hold it over our heads if we humble ourselves and ask Him for forgiveness. In the very moment we ask, Jesus will separate our offense from us. In like fashion, we can separate the offense of the person who has hurt us. Why? Because Jesus models the way for doing so.

Forgiveness is the most powerful love gift. It has the potential to build a bridge of restoration if we employ it. We can have the strength to forgive others when we remember God's forgiveness to us. This is our love gift back to God. When we operate in this merciful act, it reveals our understanding as to the depth of His gift of mercy and grace to us. Yes, we're undeserving, yet Scripture reminds us,

> But because of his great love for us, God, who is rich in mercy, made us alive with Christ even when we were dead in transgressions — it is by grace you have been saved. And God raised us up with Christ and seated us with him in the heavenly realms in

> Christ Jesus, in order that in the coming ages he might show the incomparable riches of his grace, expressed in his kindness to us in Christ Jesus. For it is by grace you have been saved, through faith—and this is not from yourselves, it is the gift of God — not by works, so that no one can boast. For we are God's handiwork, created in Christ Jesus to do good works, which God prepared in advance for us to do. (Ephesians 2:4-10)

And further, Romans 2:1-4 exhorts us,

> You, therefore, have no excuse, you who pass judgment on someone else, for at whatever point you judge another, you are condemning yourself, because you who pass judgment do the same things. Now we know that God's judgment against those who do such things is based on truth. So when you, a mere human being, pass judgment on them and yet do the same things, do you think you will escape God's judgment? Or do you show contempt for the riches of his kindness, forbearance and patience, not realizing that

> God's kindness is intended to lead you to repentance?

Truly, it's God's kindness that leads us to repentance. It's His grace, mercy and love that draw us to Him. In similar fashion, it's our kindness to those who have hurt us that can lead them to repentance and restoration—with God and with us.

We're not so ignorant to dismiss the fact that there are many who have not, and will not, respond to God's kindness and forgiveness as such. Additionally, there are some who have not, and will not, respond to our kindness and act of forgiveness as well. We have no control over how they will respond to us, and whether we'll receive an apology from them or not. The only thing we can control is our actions and our responses. We must do so as unto the Lord.

When it comes to dealing with a person who has hurt us, let's follow the way of Christ and offer forgiveness. Their reactions and the outcomes, whether good or bad, can be laid before the Lord. The rest belongs to Him. We can trust Him. We may not be able to change someone, as they are their own free moral agent, but we can choose to make a decision that can build a bridge for them to experience freedom, forgiveness, restoration and wholeness.

It's not our responsibility to rectify the injustice, nor decree the punishment on the offender. We are not asked by God to retaliate, penalize or manipulate in return. Rather, we're called to have a heart of forgiveness and move forward, even if it means knowing the individual who has caused such pain and injustice may never see their wrongdoing, change their mindset or perceptions about us.

This doesn't mean we can't establish boundaries with others. We don't have to give up our right to be emotionally, physically and spiritually safe. Forgiveness doesn't mean that we have to be vulnerable. It doesn't mean that we have to trust them. There might not even be reconciliation. Forgiveness, rather, is simply releasing them to the Lord and trusting Him to work in their lives.

So, we hold fast to our God, to His plans and to His unwavering faithfulness. We move forward emotionally and spiritually, refusing to let bitterness marinate in our hearts. We discharge any spiritual poison the enemy has tempted us to ingest in the past, and from this day forward we choose life, not death. We choose forgiveness and release, not death and bondage. We walk in freedom because He makes *all things new!*

Reflection Questions and Action Steps:

1. In what ways has this chapter influenced your thinking about forgiving others?

2. Ephesians 6:12 states, "For our struggle is not against flesh and blood, but against the rulers, against the authorities, against the powers of this dark world and against the spiritual forces of evil in the heavenly realms." How does this scripture empower you to separate the offense from the offender?

3. Is it difficult for you to separate the offense from the offender? What literal thoughts and messages does your mind rehearse when it comes to separating the offense from the offender?

4. Matthew 5:44 says, "But I tell you, love your enemies and pray for those who persecute you." Take some time to pray for those whom you see as "enemies." Though difficult, it may be the key to break you free from the hurt and bondage.

5. Take some time and write a letter offering forgiveness to the person you need to forgive. This isn't something you need to necessarily give them unless you feel the Lord prompting you to do so.

Chapter Nine
Seeking Forgiveness from Others

He sat in a corner, exhausted and disgusted at what his life had become. He had offended and failed everyone. How had he become so selfish, so consumed and so out of control? It didn't make sense, he thought. He had even been raised in a nurturing and loving home, with wealth, comfort and multiple opportunities for success, yet his life had hit rock bottom. Chaotic choices, destructive decisions, offensive actions and self-consumption had literally brought him to where he was—in the corner of a dirty pigpen.

Deeply alone, without a penny to his name and overwhelmed by hopelessness, his spiritual eyes were suddenly opened to reality. For the first time in years, he was having a spiritual awakening. Instead of dismissing the emotional moment, he began to embrace the hurt and pain he had caused so many. It was extremely difficult for him to linger in such emotions and thoughts, but he persisted. They were raw and incredibly difficult to endure. In his mind, he held steadfast to the disgust he felt for selfishly taking from and dishonoring those who had loved him the most. He wrestled with the shame he felt for willfully destroying everything good that had ever been in his life.

Instantly, a picture of his good and loving father came to mind. It was the pain he had caused his father that bothered him the most. How he wished he could go back to earlier days, earlier years. His decisions would have been virtuous, and his actions, honorable. But he couldn't go back. He could only move forward.

His dad had always been there for him, always loved him. Memories flooded his mind of just how patient, compassionate and kind his father had been in the midst of his rebellion. What he wouldn't do to take back his hurtful words and evil actions. What he wouldn't give to erase the past years and feel his father's embrace at that very moment. What he wouldn't do to be welcomed back into the safety, comfort and love of his family—to be home. Emotionally wrecked and choking with tears, he sat in isolation, groaning and sobbing.

At once, his thoughts turned into plausible action. The desire to reconcile with his father had become so strong that it was literally all he could think about. In an instant, he stood up, dusted himself off, attempted to make himself presentable and began the long journey home. With each step, he rehearsed his speech. Knowing he couldn't undo what he had already done, his words now were repentant and sorrowful. He would ask for forgiveness, and if given a chance, he would make things right.

As he rounded the corner to his home, his heart leaped. He saw his father. Thoughts flooded his mind. "What is my father thinking? What is he feeling? How will he respond to me?" Before he could ponder anymore, he saw his father sprint to him. Immediately, he fell at his father's feet. From the depths of the young man's heart and from wounds of despair, he uttered these humble and broken words, "Father, I have sinned against heaven and against you. I am no longer worthy to be called your son" (Luke 15:21).

By now, you may recognize this familiar story. It's the story of the Prodigal Son in Luke 15. And although no one prodigal story is exactly the same, we all can identify with the Biblical prodigal in that we've all offended or betrayed someone very close to us, or those around us. There's always that moment when we realize we have caused someone great pain. We might not recognize it in the actual and precise occurrence, as we might realize it much later, but there will definitely be a realization at some point in time of damage done and pain caused.

How would the story of the Prodigal Son have ended if he had not sought forgiveness and restoration from his father? Perhaps his life would have spiraled even more downhill. Perhaps both he and his father would have finished their earthly journeys with deep bitterness and regret. Perhaps they would have surrendered their life purposes to humdrum existence. The "what-ifs" are numerous and obscure, but what we do know for certain is that Jesus places a great emphasis on reconciliation—both with Him and with other people.

We've all been there. In our haste, in our immaturity, in our selfishness and more, we have hurt someone that should never have been on the receiving end of our egregious behavior. In prior chapters of this book, we've poured over scriptures about the grace and mercy of God and His forgiveness towards each one of us. We've discussed the freedom we experience when we forgive those who have hurt us, and yet there's one more element to the subject of forgiveness that is too frequently overlooked. It's the need to initiate reconciliation and forgiveness with the person we've offended and hurt. This can be a little bit harder for us to recognize, but it's imperative we address it.

Obviously, it's much easier to identify the error in another person's life and remain dismissive of our own offenses. To make this point, consider how younger children play together. Within minutes, one will see pouting, finger pointing, tears, yelling and pushing. Each child will attempt to justify why they are more right, and the other child is wrong. Fast forward to adulthood and you'll find the same thing. It's not much different; just a little more sophisticated. And if truth be told, we would much rather look at a situation and see how the other person has offended us and place all the blame on them. Yet, if we objectively look at the entire situation, we can see the part we played in the conflict. In the flesh, it's always much easier to claim, shout and pronounce that we've been victimized than to admit we have personally victimized, offended and hurt someone else.

There isn't a human being on the face of the earth who hasn't hurt and offended another person. Scripture is clear that if we have offended someone it's our responsibility to go to that person and seek amends. Restoration can occur when we initiate action to resolve the conflict. Failure to do so will result in existing barriers being fortified between us and the other person, as well as between us and God.

When we ask ourselves if there is anyone we have offended, hurt, or wronged, anyone that we need to make it right with, at least one person will usually pop into our mind. If we know this person has something against us, then this just might be the time to seek reconciliation. Pray about it.

The hurt and pain we may have inflicted on others may be a stumbling block for that person—keeping them from walking in freedom and joy. Even our inaction or our holding back may have provoked or offended. In both overt action or inaction, our offense may be causing them to live with anger, bitterness and resentment, which is inhibiting their relationship with God, us and others. Our responsibility as an ambassador of Christ is to bring reconciliation, alleviating estrangement and pursuing a genuine love for one another.

As uncomfortable as it may be for us, we need to take the time and evaluate our part in the pain we may have caused others. Our flesh often quickly rationalizes what we did and attempts to justify our actions, and yet, if we're honest with ourselves, there are those with whom we must make amends. If we error on any side, let it be to quickly apologize and seek reconciliation. As far as it depends upon us, let us take responsibility for our actions and be the bridge for restoration.

It takes deep work to search our own hearts. We usually see at a surface level and see what we want to see, not necessarily the reality of the situation. Signs always accompany offense. Perhaps the offended becomes distant. Maybe their words become more demeaning or manipulative. And even more severe, maybe they cut all ties. When signs reveal offense, we must remind ourselves of the words Jesus communicated in the Sermon on the Mount. Matthew 5:23-24 states, "Therefore, if you are offering your gift at the altar and there remember that your brother or sister has something against you, leave your gift there in front of the altar. First go and be reconciled to them; then come and offer your gift."

For Jesus, reconciliation is of upmost importance. In fact, for this very reason He came to Earth. People matter to Him. You and I matter to Him. And the person you may have offended matters to Him. As we are all handknit image-bearers of Almighty God, every unique individual has intrinsic value that should never be diminished. For this reason, Jesus implores us to reconcile with those we have offended.

As Christ followers, we are to live our lives patterned after our Savior. The entire Bible shouts out our value and worth. His mission on the earth, to seek and save the lost and to prepare a room for each of us in eternity, reveals how important we are to Him. He desires we value one another the same way. Since every human being bears the image of God, what we do to one another is really an action we appropriate as unto Him. If we hurt another person, in essence, we are hurting God as well. Simply put, we should seek forgiveness from God for hurting His image-bearers, and quickly seek forgiveness from those we have offended.

While Satan seeks to divide and destroy, God seeks to bring wholeness and restoration. Which one will we pattern our lives after? When we hurt someone, we are being destructive to an individual that God fiercely loves. His heart grieves when we don't value restoring relationships. He will always call us to repentance, forgiveness and restoration – first to Him and then to one another.

As Jesus was diligently instructing the crowds during His Sermon on the Mount, His focus was on the spirit behind the law instead of mere legalistic, mechanical actions. He always zeroed in on the heart of reconciliation. We can't just harm another image-bearer of God and go on with our "religious" ways. He wants a change in our hearts and in the way we live. He wants us to truly understand reconciliation and the freedom, healing and wholeness that comes from it.

Jesus asks us to search our hearts and to proactively take steps to right the wrongs we have done to others. He creates a pause for us as He exhorts us to first reflect on our lives before offering another "sacrifice." This allows a raw vulnerability in our hearts to remove pride, justification and selfishness. It takes down the idol of self and puts

God in His rightful place. As we quickly acknowledge our need for reconciliation with our Father, it creates a heart of repentance which brings restoration and right relationship with God and others.

So what do we do when we know we have hurt someone else and we need to make things right?

It's important to seek God's timing and approach for asking the other person to forgive us. We want to ensure our own hearts are in a stable, healthy place. A space where our words, emotions and physical disposition will bring healing and restoration. We want to have the right motives and intentions. We want to stay away from triggers, accusations, minimizing, haughtiness, wrong assumptions and a proud spirit. We want to make things better, not worse.

In seeking forgiveness, it's helpful to be specific and to go to the person with a humble heart. As we approach them in a spirit of repentance and reconciliation, we can offer an apology without justifying our actions or laying blame on the other person. We must guard our motives so that our message doesn't become, "yeah, but you ..." which will undo any sort of apology we offer.

Our steadfast commitment to the repentance and restoration process must be unwavering, even if we receive a negative response. Our hearts must stay aligned with our

Savior. Sometimes, their course of action may be to respond with anger or with more accusations. They may possibly attempt to demoralize, accuse, resist or provoke. In all of it, they are free to determine their own reactions and responses, but we must be patient and understanding, even if their responses are less than ideal.

Our response to them, in the midst of an undesirable reaction, is to be kind and loving. Immediately praying and interceding in one's spirit is always a powerful approach. Asking God to massage hearts and reconcile according to His Spirit is always edifying. These are ways of tapping into God's supernatural. Remember, a restored relationship may take some time. Trust must be rebuilt. Be okay with the process. It might take days, months or years, but trust that God is in it all.

There is so much power in living out repentance, confession and restitution.

Let's talk a bit about repentance. True repentance is turning away from sin. It's acknowledging the areas of our lives where we have done wrong to God and others, and it involves a turning away from our harmful ways. The process is turning toward correct thinking and honorable actions, in accordance with God's standards. It's useless to just feel bad about how we have treated someone and then continue to act in that same manner. This isn't true repentance. Repentance involves a change of behavior.

Confession is a powerful tool as well. It's the literal act of admitting what we've done is wrong. The enemy seeks to silence us and frequently strategizes to keep us alienated from others. Satan hates it when we boldly confess and act on God's truths. Why? Because the enemy's lies are exposed.

When we attempt to live a Godly life, and knowingly keep sin hidden in our heart, then we bring impurity into our lives and open ourselves to Satan's manipulation. But when we confess our wrongdoing, first to God and then to the ones we've hurt, we break the bondage of sin as well as the power of the enemy's attack. Satan loves to see God's children ignore tugging convictions from the Holy Spirit, and he hates it when God's children confess and seek reconciliation. Confession done God's way always brings order and makes things right.

In fact, James 5:16 says, "Therefore confess your sins to each other and pray for each other so that you may be healed. The prayer of a righteous person is powerful and effective." The power of our prayers is often tied to our repentance and confession to God, and others. This is the incredible importance God places on true restitution.

Let's recall the story in Luke 19 about the tax collector, Zacchaeus. Here was a man who used his position to take advantage of others. He would take more than the required tax amount from people while pocketing the extra money. But all that changed when he had an encounter with his Savior. When Zacchaeus was confronted by Jesus with the harm he had done to his fellow man, and then personally experienced the mercy of the Savior, he was compelled to right his wrongs. He confessed, repented and made things right. And then, he committed to giving half of all his possessions to the poor and repay anyone he had cheated, as much as four times that which he had taken.

Zacchaeus felt love and mercy from Jesus. He wanted to restore all that he had done wrong to others. We, in like fashion, because of the mercy and love we have received from Jesus, must actively seek to restore that which we have taken from others. Whether it has been through our destructive words, physical pain or something else, let us seek to restore even more than what we've taken from someone.

Seeking forgiveness from others can be a very difficult step. It must be done through prayer. Identifying God's timing and discerning His best methodology is strategic. Our purpose is to remove obstacles and barriers so reconciliation will occur. We must seek to encourage the person we have hurt. We must humble ourselves to release them from any bitterness or anger they may be holding onto. We must build a bridge of peace and follow the life-giving message of Romans 12:18, "If it is possible, as far as it depends on you, live at peace with everyone." Remember, we can only control our behavior and our decisions. As far as it depends on us, let's seek reconciliation and peace.

God loves each one of His image-bearers. He desires that we live in unity. Ephesians 4:1-3 exhorts us. "I urge you to live a life worthy of the calling you have received. Be completely humble and gentle; be patient, bearing with one another in love. Make every effort to keep the unity of the Spirit through the bond of peace."

The choice to seek forgiveness will always empower us. It will always empower others. As far as it depends on us, we must be reconciled to those in our life. For in forgiveness, we find freedom, joy and peace. Remember, He makes *all things new!*

Reflection Questions and Action Steps:

1. We've all offended and caused great emotional pain to another person in our lives at some point in time. Describe a situation in your life when you greatly hurt somebody close to you. What was the catalyst for it? Explain your mindset at the moment of the offense.

2. Offenses against others can create a lifetime of separation. What do you believe are the biggest barriers to reconciling an offense?

3. Identify a time in your life where you handled an offensive situation prayerfully. What did it look, sound and feel like? Or, identify a current situation involving you having hurt another, and describe how you might prayerfully approach restoring the relationship in the future. What would it look, sound and feel like?

4. Asking for forgiveness is empowering. Identify a person in your life who has modeled the act of asking for forgiveness appropriately and in alignment with God's Word. If you haven't seen or experienced such, what do you believe are Godly attributes that model the act of asking for forgiveness?

5. Take some time and identify the person in which you need to seek forgiveness. Spend some time in prayer and seek God as to how He wants you to rectify this situation.

SECTION FOUR
Forgiveness
Restoring Relationship with Yourself

Chapter Ten
Forgiving Yourself

"I can never forgive myself!" The more she faced her reality, the more overwhelmed she became. She groaned, cried and uttered words under her breath. Tears streamed down her face. Shame and debilitating guilt paralyzed her. She believed her life was over.

And in that very moment she decided her future. She put a stake in the ground and resolved it to be no other way. She sentenced herself to a life verdict of guilt and condemnation. She constructed a self-made prison and placed herself in solitary confinement. For the rest of her life, she would spend her time thinking about her unworthiness. She would isolate her soul into the cell of secrecy. She thought, "Forgive myself? Impossible!"

Maybe you've attached yourself to the same beliefs, for it is an all too common narrative. This destructive belief system lingers deep within so many of us. Time and time again, we've held hope that maybe there's a revelation of self-forgiveness that we haven't heard or experienced. And so, our tired souls, which so desperately crave freedom from our past, keep seeking forgiveness of self.

But here's the plot twist. God never gave us the option of forgiving oneself. There's not even Biblical precedence as such. Nowhere in the Bible does it espouse or communicate that we have the authority to forgive ourselves. There are only two types of forgiveness explained in the Bible. The first one is God forgiving us—which is vertical forgiveness, and the second one is people forgiving one another—which is horizontal forgiveness.

Look at it this way. When we say we "can't forgive ourselves" we're literally making a choice to accept or deny God's forgiveness to us—a forgiveness that is authoritative, complete, unchanging and irrefutable. We're making a choice to let the past continue to shame us, condemn us and enslave us, or we're making a choice to walk in His freedom and forgiveness. Look at what we miss out on when we dismiss His forgiveness verdict. Isaiah 43:18-19 states, "Forget the former things; do not dwell on the past. See, I am doing a new thing! Now it springs up; do you not perceive it? I am making a way in the wilderness and streams in the wasteland."

The Lord alone has created our pathway to forgiveness and restoration. He takes the broken and desolate places of our lives and brings life and hope. He is the one who offers the gift of forgiveness and creates a new life for us. Second Corinthians 5:17-18 states, "Therefore, if anyone is in Christ, the new creation has come: The old has gone, the new is here! All this is from God, who reconciled us to himself through Christ and gave us the ministry of reconciliation."

The Power of the Cross

C.S. Lewis once said, "I think that if God forgives us we must forgive ourselves. Otherwise, it is almost like setting up ourselves as a higher tribunal than Him."[5] At first glance, one will read the words of C.S. Lewis and think there's a contradiction. One may say, "You see. We must forgive ourselves."

But there's a greater depth and inference to his words. C.S. Lewis is implying there's a greater transcendence to "forgiving" oneself. Lewis is referring to final authority. He's literally saying that the highest tribunal, which is God, cannot be usurped by a lower tribunal, us. Simply stated, we don't have the authority to make a judgement call on this issue. The highest tribunal, the highest authority, however, has made the judgment call for us.

In essence—WE'RE FORGIVEN, once and for all! Look at it this way. The Supreme Court of the United States trumps all other lower court decisions and verdicts. Lower tribunals cannot usurp authority over the highest tribunal in the land. And so it is with our failures and His heavenly verdicts. If we choose to humble ourselves and ask for His forgiveness, then we are secure in His final verdict — complete and unconditional forgiveness.

When we exclaim, "I can never forgive myself," in essence, we're declaring the work Christ did on the cross as incomplete. Isn't that audacious? To believe our sin is somehow more powerful than the work of Jesus Christ's sacrifice is absolutely absurd. Our choices and past do not limit His power. The final authority is God alone, and He single-handedly conquered sin. We call Him a liar when we fail to accept His complete forgiveness. Instead, we must trust His Word and accept His verdict as supreme.

When we refuse to walk in God's forgiveness, we're choosing to live in defeat—with old thoughts, old beliefs and old defaults. However, when we realize God's forgiveness is more than enough, we open ourselves to God's transformative possibilities, endless opportunities and incredible promises. His ways are safe, refreshing, empowering, bountiful, unifying, preserving and loving. Choosing to accept and live in Christ's all-sufficient forgiveness removes unattainable attempts to forgive oneself. If we live with the false precept that "we need to forgive ourselves," we're simply denying and displacing the most cherished gift.

Think of it this way. You've been given a beautifully wrapped package, and as you pull off the bow and tear open the paper, your eyes gaze upon the most perfect gift. This has been the "thing" you have desperately wanted, hoped for and craved, more than anything else. You are overwhelmed at the generosity of the giver.

But then, your excitement turns to great sadness as a rush of thoughts course through your mind and heart. You immediately feel unworthy to receive such a priceless, sacrificial, beautiful gift. So, you put the gift in the corner, hide it away and refuse to look at it or enjoy it. Even though you yearn for the gift, time and time again, you deprive yourself of its satisfaction, beauty and pleasure. You hope and long for the day that you will feel worthy enough to enjoy the gift.

Truthfully, only Jesus could pay the price for our sins and bestow forgiveness, completely and sufficiently. Why then do we stay in the prison cell trying to forgive ourselves when He has forgiven us? Why do we stay bound to the chains of effort as if we can try harder, think harder and feel harder? The greatest "thank you" we can bestow our Savior is to accept His forgiveness, and in doing so, we reveal the glory of His gift.

In essence, God's forgiveness whispers to our hearts, "Nothing you have done has surprised me. Nothing you have done has removed you from my love. You're loved, chosen, cherished, redeemed, forgiven, restored and beautifully new. In fact, I have a new name for you. Do you know that I sing songs of love over you? I do! You're free of rejection, shame and condemnation. Let me consume your thoughts. I have a new identity for you. I have plans to prosper you beyond what you can think or imagine. And by the way, I see you as PERFECT!"

Wow! Please reread that last paragraph and let it speak to your soul.

Did you really let that soak in? Simply put, God is asking us to pivot into Him and receive His gift rather than lean into ourselves. He's asking us to pivot into His arms of grace and to respond with gratefulness and confident assurance. The pivot is to turn our back on condemnation once and for all.

When God forgives, He forgives. Period. There's no qualifier, no variable, no condition. If we ask for His forgiveness, then He forgives. He saves us from ourselves. Forever, condemnation and shame are nonexistent. We are now worthy. Unworthiness is destroyed. We are now filled with courage and faith. Hiding is no longer a coping mechanism. We are more than qualified. Feelings of disqualification are now a thing of the past. We are wholly accepted. Rejection is no longer our default. And we now walk in a new name that He has given us.

What's in a name? A name is used to identify us and to differentiate us from others. It's an identifier that tells the world who we are. All of us have names (good and bad ones) that have been given to us by our parents, by others and by the enemy. A name becomes our identity.

Negative names like Shame, Guilt, Unworthy and a host of others can easily attach themselves to our lives; yet Jesus is asking us to believe Him for the names He has given us. He's asking us to leave the old names behind and accept the following new names. Names like Redeemed, Restored, Overcomer, Chosen, Daughter of the King, Son of the Living God and New Creation. So, I ask you—what's your name?

The author of our stories, the creator of our transformation and the God of our identity reveals His incredible love for us through David's words in Psalm 139:16-17. "Your eyes saw my unformed body; all the days ordained for me were written in your book before one of them came to be. How precious to me are your thoughts, God! How vast is the sum of them!"

God holds the original pen to our story, and His storyline is perfect. Throughout life, we tend to take the pen from His hand and attempt to write out our own story. No matter how far we go in the process, He is always waiting for us to hand Him back the pen. He is the God of reversals and renewals. As we see the nature of God woven through each book, each chapter, each verse and each word in the Bible, we can trust in His authorship, and ultimately, in the outcomes He so desires for us.

I've often thought God's divine and sovereign providence has placed us in our unique places on planet earth. It's in these very spheres of influence, in this current dispensation, in our ethnic personhood and in our cultural settings, even in our families and even in our circumstances, so that we might fully know Him—as much as possible this side of heaven. One day we will see Him fully and what a wonderful day that will be, but in the meantime we see dimly. Seeing dimly is His sovereign will at this time, but even in this, we can trust His mercy, grace and love to author our lives.

He's written our stories so we may reveal His glory in this world. Even in our rebellion and mistakes, though not designed by Him, He is constantly at work with the pen. The ink is bright and bold when He writes in the grace and mercy portions to our stories. Ephesians 2:4-5 states,

"But because of His great love for us, God, who is rich in mercy, made us alive with Christ even when we were dead in transgressions—it is by grace you have been saved."

Read the words of His authorship to His chosen people. Listen to the very names He gives them. Relish in His beautiful character and nature. Delight in the outcomes He bestows them. Isaiah 62:1-5 says,

> For Zion's sake I will not keep silent, for Jerusalem's sake I will not remain quiet, till her vindication shines out like the dawn, her salvation like a blazing torch. The nations will see your vindication, and all kings your glory; you will be called by a new name that the mouth of the Lord will bestow. You will be a crown of splendor in the Lord's hand, a royal diadem in the hand of your God. No longer will they call you Deserted, or name your land Desolate. But you will be called Hephzibah (meaning "my delight is in her"), and your land Beulah (meaning "married"); for the Lord will take delight in you, and your land will be married. As a young man marries a young woman, so will your Builder marry

you; as a bridegroom rejoices over his bride,
so will your God rejoice over you.

Our Heavenly Father says, "My delight is in her." What's her name? Her name is Delightful. He speaks His words to us and tells us that He rejoices over us, just like a faithful groom would say and do for his bride.

In Christ, we're restored and redeemed. Destructive names and labels are destroyed. Why? Because we are crowned in His righteousness. The enemy doesn't want us to walk with this new identity, new power and new name. He would rather us focus on feelings of desperation, purposelessness and hopelessness. He wants us to pick up the pen and write the life we were never meant to author.

We are released from our self-made prison cell. The door is wide open and we are liberated. The chains have been removed and we are free. We are holy, righteous and redeemed. God has freed us! We now walk in joy, hope and peace. He makes *all things new!*

Reflection Questions and Action Steps:

1. Do you feel as if you must forgive yourself before you can move forward in your life? Why or why not? How is this an unbiblical concept?

2. In what areas of your life do you find yourself dwelling on the past and not accepting God's forgiveness? How has your life been in a wilderness or wasteland? How is God changing your identity and perceptions?

3. In 2 Corinthians 5:17-18 it states, "Therefore, if anyone is in Christ, the new creation has come: The old has gone, the new is here! All this is from God, who reconciled us to himself through Christ and gave us the ministry of reconciliation." God's promises are faithful, always and forever. After reading this passage, what steps come to mind as to how you can move forward in the reality of a new, abundant life?

4. Names are identifiers and every name has a meaning. What name (or identifying characteristics) do you feel you have given yourself and what name (or identifying characteristics) do you feel God is giving you?

5. Spend some time and write a prayer of gratitude and acceptance for the sufficiency of Christ's forgiveness over every sin, failure and fear in your life.

Chapter Eleven
Truth Over Feelings

Feelings are a beautiful part of our humanity. Through them, we express and experience empathy, compassion, love, justice, sadness, anger and much more. Feelings keep us from being mechanistic, robotic and soulless. And feelings frequently act as catalysts for meaning, connection and intimacy.

Feelings are not in and of themselves wrong. God created feelings for you and me to know the deepest forms of love, and to experience wholeness. Yet, feelings can be triggers for deep pain and disconnectedness. Additionally, they can be altogether subjective and can even lead us to return to feelings of unworthiness, even after we've experienced complete forgiveness from God.

In the previous chapters, we explored God's forgiveness for us, our forgiveness toward others, asking others to forgive us and the idea of forgiving oneself. In the process, we were reminded of God's truths. We even delved into Scripture passages extolling our right standing with God, where we acknowledge His forgiveness and accept His grace.

Yet, life happens. Feelings come and feelings go. They often become a deceptive trap that takes truth into captivity. Left unchecked, feelings can lead to a false reality and a misperception of the truth. History is filled with individuals making extremely poor decisions due to run away feelings that have led them down a destructive path.

Feelings have a way of leading us astray unless carefully matched up against an objective truth and in light of God's standards. The cultural mantra of "following our own truth" will always wreak havoc in our lives if we choose to oblige. But God's truths, His unchanging Word, is true 100% of the time. It is never partially true or sometimes false. It transcends the test of time, and it transcends the test of feelings. It's as true as true gets.

What happens when feelings overwhelm what we know to be true according to Scripture?

There was a powerful United States military leader in the late 1700s to early 1800s. His name was General William Hull. With impressive credentials as a military leader, judge, senator and governor, Hull's life came to a crossroads during the War of 1812. Known for his strong leadership and vast experience, he was a natural choice to lead the invasion into Canada with the hopes of quickly halting the war.

As Hull and his soldiers began advancing into Canadian territory, he became fearful and uncertain of his next steps. Overwhelming feelings of possible defeat washed over him and weakened his resolve to win the battle. Further compounding his fears, Hull learned the enemy had captured a vessel containing the description of his battle plan and journal writings. In them were notations acknowledging his fears at having to face the British and Indian forces.

Hull's opposition was led by British General Isaac Brock, and Tecumseh, the Shawnee Indian Chief. If one looked purely at numbers, the British and Indian forces were outnumbered by Hull and the American soldiers. It was said that Brock's troops consisted of only 300 British soldiers, 400 Canadian militiamen and 600 Indians. Hull's troops, however, numbered 2,000 and were highly experienced and trained.

General Brock wrote a fake letter, which he made sure was intercepted by the Americans. In it, Brock deceptively boasted of having 5,000 Natives at his disposal to fight a battle against Hull. Further adding to Hull's fear, Brock wrote another misleading letter and sent it directly to Hull. In it, he warned that he feared he would be unable to control the Indians' intense and bloody fighting once the battle ensued.

General Brock then followed his words with deceptive action. With great trickery, Brock had Tecumseh, the Shawnee Chief, instruct the Indians to march multiple times past the fort, giving the appearance there were more of them than there really were. Also, Brock had the Canadians dress in old British uniforms to give the appearance that the British army was much larger than it was in reality.

Brock's tactics successfully wreaked havoc with Hull. Feelings of fear and dread swept over him. The momentous decision he faced came front and center. Would Hull rely on his feelings or would he make a decision based upon truth?

The reality was that General Hull had great military experience. His soldiers were well trained. The Americans were a solid force and were prepared for battle. Yet, Hull held on to his feelings. History would record that with just a few shots fired by the British, General Brock immediately called for General Hull to surrender. And surprisingly to everyone, Hull surrendered without even a fight. Talk about the power of feelings.[6]

Like Hull, how many times do we let our feelings create a false reality? How many times do we let our feelings determine our life choices and responses? How often do our feelings draw us back into the dark areas of regret, shame, guilt, condemnation and more? Why do we pivot from the truth of Scripture?

Early one morning, my husband and I went out for a run in our neighborhood. It was still dark outside and my eyesight wasn't very good without my contacts. As it was still early, I chose not to wear my contacts and knew everything would look like a large, blurry blob. On the return route home, I was peacefully running along in the quietness of the dark morning, allowing my mind to formulate my plans for the day when out from nowhere—with absolutely no warning and no preparation—I found myself facedown on the pavement. I was stunned. I had no idea how I ended up on the ground. One moment I was running and within a split second I had faceplanted onto the hard pavement. As I pulled myself up, with my pride hurt more than anything else, I looked back and saw a small bump in the asphalt. Due to darkness and poor eyesight, I failed to see what "cut in on my race" home.

In many ways, that's the power of negative feelings cutting in, interrupting and bringing us down. Sometimes we can handle them just fine, but on other days they can bring out the worst in us. Perhaps it's past memories that rush in, or feelings of regret and unworthiness. We may even wonder how we ended up in that dark place in our mind again, just when we thought we were successfully moving forward.

In Galatians 5:7-9, Paul compares our life journey to a race. He says, "You were running a good race. Who cut in on you to keep you from obeying the truth? That kind of persuasion does not come from the one who calls you. 'A little yeast works through the whole batch of dough.'"

What are the triggers that are persuading us, that are wanting to cut in on our life race, our life journey? What are those false realities that are distracting and disabling? What are the errant feelings we're holding onto that are throwing us into a tailspin? What emotions are causing us to revisit those areas where we've already experienced forgiveness and healing? Why is shame, regret and condemnation coming back?

It's the little bumps in our journey that will slow our progress, disorient us or inhibit us from living fully alive. Paul points out we can be deterred by influential thoughts and feelings. He even states that a little bit of yeast affects the entirety of a loaf of bread, and so do thoughts and feelings. When we allow little, negative thoughts into our hearts and minds, then they can affect us in exponential fashion, just like yeast in bread. Whatever we put into our hearts and minds, no matter how small, has the ability to multiply in quantity and quality.

In order to not allow comments, personal memories or even our own misguided thoughts to cut in on our race, we must see clearly, objectively and in line with God's truths. Through consistent Bible study, Scripture memorization, meditation on God's truth, prayer and Christian fellowship, we can run the good race and counter wayward thoughts and feelings.

Honestly, I probably wouldn't have tripped and fallen flat on my face when I was jogging if it had been daylight and I had been wearing my contacts. I would have been able to see more clearly. Likewise, we need the application of God's truths to help us see clearly and to avoid having our feelings trip us up.

Romans 12:2 says, "Do not conform to the pattern of this world, but be transformed by the renewing of your mind. Then you will be able to test and approve what God's will is – His good, pleasing and perfect will." Instead of thinking and reacting as someone whose ideas come from the world, we can renew our minds in God's truths. Having the mind of Christ in our beliefs and actions is transformative and powerful. Our beliefs, decision making and life purposes must be found in and through Jesus Christ.

Truth is such a gracious gift bestowed to us by the Father. The enemy would have us believe truth is fluid, and that feelings determine what is true for each person. This lie leads to despair and hopelessness. Jesus said in John 8:32, "Then you will know the truth, and the truth will set you free." Freedom comes when we live in truth and truth can only come from our Heavenly Father.

Scripture tells us we live in a spiritual battle that is often unseen, but felt in our everyday lives. Recalling the account of God's pronouncement to Satan in Genesis 3, the Lord said the enemy would strike our heel, but we would crush his head. The enemy is constantly nipping at our heels and we often allow him territory into our thoughts and feelings when he has no right. Feelings can betray us, but truth will set us free.

There is a great battle for truth, for truth begets freedom. Ephesians 6:10-18a describes how we are to arm ourselves in order to be victorious.

> Finally, be strong in the Lord and in his mighty power. Put on the full armor of God, so that you can take your stand against the devil's schemes. For our struggle is not against flesh and blood, but against the rulers, against the authorities, against the powers of this dark world and against the spiritual forces of evil in the heavenly realms. Therefore put on the full armor of God, so

> that when the day of evil comes, you may be able to stand your ground, and after you have done everything, to stand. Stand firm then, with the belt of truth buckled around your waist, with the breastplate of righteousness in place, and with your feet fitted with the readiness that comes from the gospel of peace. In addition to all this, take up the shield of faith, with which you can extinguish all the flaming arrows of the evil one. Take the helmet of salvation and the sword of the Spirit, which is the word of God. And pray in the Spirit on all occasions with all kinds of prayers and requests."

Our strength to live an overcoming life comes solely through God. He has given us the tools to arm ourselves against the lies and attacks of the enemy. Through His gift of this spiritual armor, we can stand firm and not be swayed by negative thoughts, unchecked feelings, words of others, past memories and more. Entire studies have been done on the armor of God and it is worth our time to dive deeper into studying this, but for now, let's touch very briefly on each piece of armor.

Belt of Truth

Truth is what holds everything together. Without it, our lives will fall apart and we will live in a state of chaos and confusion, being tossed and turned by any new thoughts, ideas or feelings. Living in God's truth is what brings us strength to combat destructive lies and ideas, and keeps us on the right path.

Breastplate of Righteousness

The breastplate protects our heart and other vital organs. Being covered in God's righteousness will stop harmful tactics of the enemy that are trying to make us feel unworthy, condemned and unloved. We put on our breastplate of righteousness in order to protect our hearts and feelings.

Shoes of the Gospel of Peace

Everywhere we go, we carry with us the gospel of peace. Peace comes to us by living restored with our Savior. We are not enemies of God, but we are His children. As God fills our hearts, thoughts and feelings with peace, we carry it wherever we go. Second Thessalonians 3:16 states, "Now may the Lord of peace himself give you peace at all times and in every way."

Shield of Faith

By faith, we believe what Jesus says about us being totally and completely forgiven. This enables us to dismiss the triggers and even the feelings of our past that threaten to disable us. We can live by faith when we hold the shield. Faith allows us to trust what God decrees over our lives is true, and faith protects us from the assaults of the enemy's lies.

Helmet of Salvation

When the enemy's lies threaten to bring doubt of our salvation and redemption, the helmet of salvation will guard our thoughts and minds, thus keeping the power of the lies at bay. Additionally, the helmet of salvation is the added assurance we need when the feelings of despair and despondency attempt to sabotage the truth.

Sword of the Spirit

The Sword of the Spirit is our offensive weapon empowering us to wield God's truth. Swords slash and penetrate—they attack. As our position in Christ is that of a warrior, we can attack the enemy's voice and tactics by utilizing the sword of God's truth, power and presence.

Prayer

The Holy Spirit was given to us to be our advocate, teacher, counselor and guide. John 16:13a says, "But when he, the Spirit of truth comes, he will guide you into all the truth." The Holy Spirit, through our prayer and intercession, aligns our minds and hearts to God's truth, His will and to the divine destiny He has chosen for us.

Daily fitting ourselves with the armor of God will empower us to walk in truth and align our feelings with God's Word. The Lord wants us to confidently walk in our position as His sons and daughters, and confidence is assured when we have on the armor of God. First John 3:19-21 states, "This is how we know that we belong to the truth and how we set our hearts at rest in his presence: If our hearts condemn us, we know that God is greater than our hearts, and he knows everything. Dear friends, if our hearts do not condemn us, we have confidence before God."

If we want the freedom, power and confidence that are revealed in the aforementioned passage, then we must take hold by believing and applying His truths. Living in truth equates to believing what God says, and it's important to remember that we can't pick and choose what we believe in the Bible. Either it's entirely true, or it's not.

Believing the truth about our identity in Christ and His redemptive character must be enshrined in our mindset. Sometimes, all we can do when negative feelings and emotions flood us is initiate thoughts of faith and truth. When God says we're a new creation in Christ, and that the past is gone and the new has come (2 Corinthians 5:17), then we must stand upon this pure, empirical and transformational truth. When God declares we are righteous and we walk as His sons and daughters, then we must cast out all fears, doubts and regrets, and walk as the royal children He created us to be. If He says it, then we must believe it.

But how are we to set our hearts at rest in His presence when we feel so condemned, hurt and ashamed?

First and foremost, condemnation doesn't come from the Father, but conviction does. It's important to discern the difference. Condemnation is shame, but conviction is positive correction. Secondly, when one is at rest with someone, the individual has the freedom to be themselves. With God, we can let our guard down and trust that we will be received and loved, no matter the situation. Lastly, setting our hearts at rest in His presence means we can come boldly before God, with full confidence, and talk to Him about everything and anything. He longs for His children to be honest, and He longs for His children to cherish His ways. If our hearts perpetually condemn us, then we must counter the thoughts and feelings with the truth that God is greater than our hearts—that His sovereignty trumps all fleshly thoughts and emotions.

When condemnation manifests in our hearts, we are forced to either hide in an emotional stronghold or run into a dark space of hopelessness. Sometimes we are tempted to hide in a fortress of fear and blame, and other times we sprint into hostility, only to hasten blame. In all, a downward spiral of negativities and bondage will manifest.

John 3:17 says, "For God did not send his Son into the world to condemn the world, but to save the world through him." Romans 8:1 says, "Therefore, there is now no condemnation for those who are in Christ Jesus, because through Christ Jesus the law of the spirit who gives life has set you free from the law of sin and death." In Christ there is no condemnation, therefore, we must not condemn ourselves.

First John 3:20 asserts that "God is greater than our hearts and he knows everything." He knows all we do, think and say, and yet He still chose to die on the cross and pay the price for our sin. If we perpetuate self-condemnation, we forfeit our freedom. God knows every part of our hearts, even better than we do. Since God knows the good, bad and ugly in our hearts, and freely offers complete freedom and restoration when we repent, then we must choose not to walk in condemnation.

Rather than walking in self-condemnation, God allows us to walk confidently. As we choose to believe God's truth about our right standing with Him, we can walk securely in Him and upright before others. Confidence can be seen as unwavering, fearless and unhesitating faith in communion with God. This treasure of truth reveals the removal of fear and anxiety which characterizes mankind's relationship to God. It comes as the result of guilt being set aside by the power of the cross.

What a gift it is to walk fearlessly, without hesitation, completely in His love. And this is what we receive when we respond to Him like an earthly child running unhesitatingly into their loving father's arms. It's straightforward. We can choose condemnation, or we can choose freedom. It truly is a decision of the heart. Philippians 3:13 states, "Brothers and sisters, I do not consider myself yet to have taken hold of it. But one thing I do: Forgetting what is behind and straining toward what is ahead, I press on toward the goal to win the prize for which God has called me heavenward in Christ Jesus."

Accepting the fullness and completeness of His forgiveness allows us to rejoice in Him, and cherish His goodness. Jesus said in John 8:32, "Then you will know the truth, and the truth will set you free." When we hold fiercely to His truth, then we walk with victory over shame and condemnation. Remember, He makes *all things new!*

Reflection Questions and Action Steps:

1. What are the things that trigger unchecked feelings in your life? From truths found in this chapter, communicate a possible intervention or solution.

2. What, if anything, is keeping you from experiencing God's total and complete forgiveness? Or, what has been a struggle for most people in understanding God's forgiveness?

3. Identify a piece of armor that has great meaning to you. Explain how it is, or could be, greatly beneficial to you in this next chapter of your life.

4. Summarize the entirety of this chapter into two power sentences. In so doing, you might ask and answer the following question, "What is the greatest takeaway from this chapter?

5. It's important to be able to identify what triggers us in order to create a game plan to counteract such triggers. Take some time to identify some practical actions that can cause you to check your feelings so you can walk in truth and freedom. How will this look?

Chapter Twelve
The New You

My husband and I travel to Goma, Democratic Republic of Congo (DRC) several times each year. DRC is one of the poorest countries in the world at any given time. Through our nonprofit, Legacy Incorporated, we focus on helping victimized women, widows and orphans. On the outskirts of Goma is a former refugee camp. Many people have called this place home even in the midst of two major Congolese wars, countless insurrections and the Rwandan genocide. The camp, just outside of Goma, is called Mugunga.

The people we've met in Mugunga are beautiful—on the inside and out. And although they've experienced great difficulties and tremendous tragedy, each time we visit they welcome us with open arms and open hearts. It truly is an honor to know them and to be known by them.

While the people are amazing and the country is exquisite, there's a definite challenge in getting in and out of the country. On one recent visit, we had a complicated time boarding the airplane to return home. It was post-Covid, things were slowly opening up with less restrictions, but the United States was still requiring a negative Covid test to be taken 24 hours before boarding the return flight.

Being proactive, we checked with the DRC's testing availability and found that they only offered testing 48 hours in advance. That wasn't going to work in order for us to meet the United States' requirements. But we soon learned that we could preorder Covid-19 test kits in the U.S., carry them with us to the DRC, and utilize them via a Telehealth app in order to meet the 24 hour timeframe. We thought we had an effective solution, so off we went.

The trip was successful and all went as planned. On the last day, just 24 hours before our return flight home, we took our tests. The results were negative, and we proceeded to arrive at the airport the next morning with the results in hand.

As soon as we arrived, we approached an employee at the airport terminal entrance. When we showed him our documents, one of which was the Covid test results, he refused to let us proceed. We were greatly surprised. The individual was adamant in his refusal. He stated that we had to take the mandated DRC Covid test and that our negative Covid test results were not sufficient.

Even after our explanation of the facts, the individual refused to accept the results of our Telehealth test. He proceeded to tell us that we would have to drive across town to take the tests, pay for them out of pocket, but not to worry, because we would have the results back within an hour. We knew right then and there that our flight home was in jeopardy. Just the time it would take to drive across town, with all of the traffic, could preclude us from boarding the plane on time. We were in a quagmire but the employee was not budging. He offered no other solution.

Frustrated, knowing this was inaccurate information, we drove across town to the so-called "official" testing site. Upon arriving, we were advised that there was no way we would get our results within an hour. They told us it would be more like two hours at the soonest. Quickly, we drove back to the airport hoping we could persuade the airport personnel into accepting our U.S. approved tests. Still, no budging. But as our translator was communicating with the person who had sent us away the first time, we prayed for a breakthrough. After their ten minute conversation, and a hidden exchange of one hundred dollars, we were finally allowed to proceed to the next station, eventually boarding the plane.

As we settled into our seats for the two and a half hour flight to Ethiopia, a two hour layover and another seventeen hour flight en route to Chicago, I found myself sandwiched between the two biggest men on the plane. One was my broad shouldered husband. The other was a large Congolese man whose legs took up all of his seat and a third of mine. I took a deep breath, said a prayer and hunkered down for the flight. You might be asking, "How did it go? Were you miserable? Did your muscles cramp? Were you exhausted?"

Absolutely! In every way!

When we finally arrived to Chicago, we found our way to the Global Entry kiosk. Global Entry allows individuals to expedite their way through Customs and Immigration. It's a little work up front, and a few dollars beforehand, but it's worth it in the end because it saves you so much time. Generally, when returning from out of the country, we simply avoid the lines, walk up to a kiosk, have our picture taken and the machine prints out an acceptance receipt which we take to the security officer. And then we proceed. It's that easy.

Everything went well at first. I observed that my husband had taken his picture and immediately received his confirmation receipt. Simple and easy. Then, it was my turn. So I confidently walked up to the kiosk and took my picture, but no receipt was given. I was confused. I proceeded to follow the kiosk instructions and scanned my passport. Still, no receipt. Then I proceeded to add all the identifying markers to show the kiosk that it was really me. Finally, after a lengthy process, the machine distributed an acceptance receipt, and I handed it to the Customs' officer.

Honestly, I was a bit confused. I thought, "Why did my husband get through so quickly, but why did I have to go through all of the extra steps to prove my identity?" As I left security, I went into the bathroom, and it was there that I had a sudden realization. I looked into the mirror and I could barely recognize my haggard self. I thought and said out loud, "Oooohhh, that's why!" I looked terrible! So bad, in fact, that the state-of-the-art Global Entry kiosk couldn't recognize me. Whether that was the reason or not, it would be hard to convince me otherwise. I looked like I had been to war and back.

This funny little story packs a meaningful punch when it comes to the subject of identity. Think about it. Regardless of how I looked, I was still me. There were personal identifiers about me as I stood in front of the kiosk, beyond the limited perspective of the camera. Even if the kiosk didn't recognize me, I was still me. And regardless of how I felt after the flight, I was still me. I was the one and only, Cheryl Braden, in all the world, despite my identity being momentarily denied.

This is true of our identity in Christ as well. God, our Creator, handcrafted us to be the unique person we are, and He calls us to live in the identity He has defined for us. Our journeys may have been a bit rough. Life may have gotten a bit messy and has not gone the way we've planned, yet through Christ, God gives us the identity He created for us to live.

Just 24 hours after the flight, I began to look like my true self again—thanks to sleep, food and a shower. My identity had not changed. And so it is with life. There may be things in our lives that we need to clean up, and we may need to amend some choices, actions and priorities to bring them into alignment with God's beautiful standards, but our identity in Christ is always secure and immovable.

As we've arrived at our final chapter together, I'm reminded that we've worked through understanding God's great love and forgiveness for us, the need to forgive others, the errant belief of forgiving ourselves and the power of aligning our feelings with truth. But to intentionally move forward, we must understand and live out our true identity in Christ.

My dear one, may I have a moment where my heart can speak deeply to yours?

So much happens in this life journey that attempts to define who you are. I see it in your face. You carry insecurity, doubt, shame, guilt, sorrow, confusion, frustration, hopelessness and more. God never intended you to live that way. He had, or should I say has, so much more for you. Don't listen to the lies that have been spoken over you. Don't listen to the reminders of your regretful decisions. And, don't let your past pain define you.

As you walk from repentance to salvation, you've been ushered into redemption and wholeness. From the beginning of time your loving Creator sculpted your very being into existence. There was no mistake. You are no accident. You were uniquely destined to live your life as an honored image-bearer of the Almighty God. You were destined to shine, so when people see your life, they will be introduced to the glory of God. Your identity does not come from what you have or have not done. Your identity does not come from what you feel. Your true identity can only come from your Creator.

How your Heavenly Father longs to pull you into His loving arms, wipe away every tear, every hurt, every feeling of shame and guilt, and restore you to His righteousness. He patiently waits for you to seek Him and allow Him to reshape you into the individual you were created to be. Don't fear Him, don't run from Him, for He is so very good. He delights in you and longs to see you walk into the beautiful purposes He has for you. As your Creator, He knows you better than you know yourself. He knows what you need and what your heart truly longs for. Trust Him. Open your heart completely to Him and watch as He gently reminds you of your true identity.

Why Your Identity Matters

The questions we ask one another are often generic and formulaic when we meet someone for the first time. They often sound like this: What do you do for a living? Where do you go to school? Where do you live? What do you like to do for fun? People often gauge who we are and what type of person we are by what we do, so it makes sense that our perceived validation comes by what we do or who we're associated with. This becomes our perceived identity—who we think we are.

The enemy of our souls would like to give us our identity by what we have done in the past — our mistakes, failures and hurts. He wants us to be defined by shame, guilt and pain. He wants us to believe that we're unlovable, irredeemable and unable. He frequently uses others to help mold, shape and define our identities so as to structure the way we see ourselves and our circumstances. And yet, God is calling us to live in our true identity.

Knowing and walking in our true identity affects every aspect of our lives. Our perceived identity determines what we believe, the decisions and choices we make, what we care about, how we choose to live our lives, and more. If we understand that we are priceless, a chosen daughter or son of the King, we will make decisions that bring value to ourselves and others. In contrast, if we believe we are one big mistake, we will make decisions that devalue and destroy us, and others.

There's an identity crisis in this world today. We see God's children rapidly straying far from His identity and attempting to define and identify themselves in all the ways they were never intended. Running from God truths, many are finding themselves jumping from one identity to the next—aimlessly attempting to understand who they are. This confusion and hopelessness can be rectified, however, when we align ourselves to our identity in Christ.

Jesus Christ alone has given us our true identity. When known and realized, we experience freedom, joy, peace and empowerment. True identity can be found nowhere else, and in no one else. It can only be found in Him. We read in 2 Corinthians 5:17, "Therefore, if anyone is IN Christ, the new creation has come: The old has gone, the new is here!"

The power to change and live securely in our identity in Christ comes with that simple word – IN. The secret is in the continual living and abiding in Christ where His healing power and truth instructs our hearts, minds and souls. It's our Heavenly Father telling us who we are, what we mean to Him and who we were always meant to be. Because we are in Christ, our past does not have to dictate who we are. In Christ, words from others can bounce right off us. In Christ, our identity is solely defined by the One who knows and loves us best.

Foundation of Your Identity

Jesus tells a parable in Matthew 7:24-27 about the wise and foolish man. He said:

> Therefore everyone who hears these words of mine and puts them into practice is like a wise man who built his house on the rock. The rain came down, the streams rose, and the winds blew and beat against that house; yet it did not fall, because it had its foundation on the rock. But everyone who hears these words of mine and does not put them into practice is like a foolish man who built his house on sand. The rain came down, the

streams rose, and the winds blew and beat against that house, and it fell with a great crash.

What foundation is our identity built on? Is it on the unchanging, solid truths of God or is it on the ever-shifting thoughts and ideas of the culture, and those around us? Do we find ourselves crumbling in every storm that passes through our life, or do we find ourselves stronger, more secure and more at peace even as we're buffeted by the seasons of life? Here are three questions to ask ourselves in determining where the foundations of our identity lie.

1. Whose voices are we listening to?

2. What are the voices saying?

3. What are our responses to what the voices are saying?

Whose voices are we listening to?

Voices, noise and distractions are everywhere. It's difficult to get to a quiet place. The voices of friends, family, co-workers, adversaries and even our own self-talk influence us in a certain way and steer us in a particular direction. How are we to live in a world with so many voices, so many ideas and so many agendas competing to identify us? How can we rest securely in God's identity for us and who He has made us to be? Is God's voice supreme in our lives?

What are the voices saying?

There's an old fable told through the ages that speaks to the power of voices.

One day, there was a farmer who discovered an eagle's egg on the ground. Kindly, he stooped to retrieve the egg and placed it with his chickens. In this way, it had a chance to survive. As time passed, the eagle's egg hatched along with the other chicken eggs. The eagle was born and raised along with the other chickens, and not knowing anything other than his environment, he began to do the things chickens do.

The young eagle spent his days scratching in the dirt for food, never really flying more than the occasional chicken hop, and running in fear of everything around him. One day, as he was outside with his chicken friends and family, the young eagle saw a majestic bird flying high in the sky. Amazed at the beauty, brilliance and strong nature of the bird flying so elegantly, he asked a chicken what he was seeing.

The chicken replied, "Why, that's a great eagle! The King of all the birds! He belongs to the sky, but we chickens belong to the ground. You can never be that." Sadly, the young eagle watched as the great eagle in the sky soared away at a great distance. Then the young eagle lowered his gaze, went back to scratching in the dirt, and settled for a humdrum existence because he believed that he was a chicken and destined for a chicken's existence.

Like the young eagle who thought he was a chicken, so much of our life is spent not knowing who we truly are and what we were created to do. Like the young eagle, we find ourselves thinking, believing and behaving like those around us. We grow accustomed to listening to the wrong voices and failing to act in accordance with what we were created for.

We were made to soar! Like the young eagle, we were made for so much more. We live differently when we understand our identity as a daughter or son of the King of kings. Why are we satisfied with scratching in the dirt for our sustenance? Why are we just believing that is all there is to our lives? Which voices told us that we should settle for less than what we were created for? Who told us we weren't worth more and destined for more?

But listen to God's voice in 1 Peter 2:9, "But you are a chosen people, a royal priesthood, a holy nation, God's special possession, that you may declare the praises of him who called you out of darkness into his wonderful light."

We are chosen. We are not an accident. We are not a copy. We are a one-of-a-kind original who has been purposefully handmade by our loving Creator. We have been chosen. Even though our past and the voices around us speak messages that cause us to believe we're unlovable and useless, our God absolutely adores us. Even though we hear messages that we're a "throw-away" and nothing special, even worthless, our Creator says the opposite. He is absolutely enthralled with us and loves us with an everlasting love!

We are His royal sons and daughters. When a person is from a royal family, they walk differently, talk differently, behave differently and make decisions differently. They know there is a responsibility to carry the family name. With the name comes authority and position. Remember the Zechariah 3:6-7 passage we discussed earlier? When the Lord forgives us and we walk in obedience, He gives us a position of governing with Him. We were born to be His sons and daughters and walk in royalty.

We are holy. Because of Jesus' sacrifice on the cross, we are holy, set apart from the world, for good works – set apart to live according to His standards. Jesus calls us to a better life. We were not destined for garbage. We were not created to just survive. We were created for so much more.

We are valuable, and living a holy life comes with living in Christ. He alone cleanses us and gives us the ability to make decisions that honor God.

We are special. Most of us have a special item that means more to us than anything else. We protect it, cherish it and value it above all else. God says we are His special possession. He values us, cherishes us, loves us and cares for us.

We bring good news of our great God. We have the amazing opportunity to respond to the Lord in gratefulness for who He is and of His great love for us. We get to testify to the world of His goodness, of His love and of His redemption for mankind.

We are in the light. We were never meant to live in darkness. Darkness is for those who fear, those who hurt and hurt others, those living in shame and guilt, those who think of evil and not goodness, those who are trapped and those who feel unworthy. God has called us into light. He has called us to be where He is. He stepped into the darkness to rescue and redeem us. We were meant to live in His light for eternity.

God has called us to stop scratching in the dirt and living satisfied with worldly scraps. He has called us to look up and soar. When we listen to the voice of God, and what

He speaks over our lives, then we will live a life greater than we could ever imagine.

We are unique, a one-of-a-kind creation, filled with purpose and intention. We are not an accident. We are not disposable. Our identity is defined by who God says we are and whose we are. God is not glorified by us living less than our best. The greatest thanks we can offer our Savior for His sacrifice on the cross is to live our lives the way He created us to live.

On the contrary, our archnemesis (Satan), would love nothing more than for you and me to walk opposed to our identity in Christ. He does not want us to understand who God made us to be. When we allow anyone other than God to determine our identity, we begin to fade away from who we were intended to be. It's like someone has painted over the masterpiece that we are and is giving us a new image, instead of bearing the image of God. The Master Artist created each one of us as beautiful art. We are His expression of His love to the world, but sin paints over God's masterpiece until the original artwork becomes invisible and something far inferior becomes visible.

Several years ago in Paris, France, construction workers were removing a wall in a former insurance agency in order to create a beautiful boutique for the Oscar de la Renta clothing line. As the workers were removing pieces of particle board, they were shocked to discover a large 10-foot x 20-foot canvas painting glued to a hidden wall. As art restorers were called in, and the grime and old varnish were removed, they discovered a 17th century masterpiece created by famed artist, Arnould de Vuez. It was a hidden painting that was one of four that had been commissioned to portray the travels of Louis XIV's ambassador to the Middle East. No one knew the story of how this painting ended up where it was or why it was hidden there for so many years. Amazing! It's uncanny to think just how many times people walked past the cheap particle board wall not knowing that a great masterpiece was lying behind. It was in their very presence the entire time.[7]

This story has multiple implications and lessons for our own lives. Who have we allowed to cover up our intended identity? What words and messages have they created and scribbled? What past decisions have we made that put cheap particle board over our beauty?

God, the ultimate Creator, handknit us together into a perfect masterpiece, but over the years, through our decisions and the choices of others, His work of art has slowly been covered up until the beauty of what we were intended to be, and to reveal, has become hidden. I'm so thankful that the Divine Art Restorer removes the cheap layer coverings of our lives, brushes off the dirt and grime, and reinstates the beauty of the original masterpiece—our true identity.

We are not our past circumstances nor are we what others have tried to make us to be. We are not our thoughts and feelings. The result of walking in forgiveness from God is a restoration of our true identity. When we live with our identity solely rooted in the truth of Jesus Christ, we will no longer seek approval and validation from others. God is our Creator. Only He is the One who has the right and authority to name us, to identify us.

Perusing the Scriptures, we read from history how God has called out the true identities of His creation. Here are just a few examples:

Abraham – from childlessness to father of many nations

Gideon – from hiding in fear from the Midianites to Mighty Warrior

David – from having a wandering heart to a man after God's own heart

Peter – from a brash, emotional man to a steady rock on which Christ built His church

Paul – from a persecutor of Christians to a great apostle who wrote over half of the New Testament

Samaritan Woman – from a woman hiding in shame to a bold evangelist

Mary Magdalene – from a woman who was filled with seven demons to an ambassador of Christ filled with the Holy Spirit

Zacchaeus – from a tax collector lacking integrity and taking from others to a man with great integrity and generosity

Rahab – from a prostitute to a woman of honor through whom King David and Jesus descended

Joseph – from being rejected by family and being a prisoner to being the second in command of Egypt

And what about you? What is God speaking over you? Who is He calling you to be? What does it look like for you to live out your identity in Christ?

What are our responses to what the voices are saying?

Voices are many. Their messages about us are loud and clear, but how we respond to them dictates the rest of our life. People will always have perceptions and opinions about us. They will misunderstand us. We will even get "those" looks, reactions and comments. Greater yet, they will work hard to pull us back into the chicken coop and convince us we're only destined for humdrum existence, not soaring. What will our response be?

Psalm 103:11-12 reminds us, "For as high as the heavens are above the earth, so great is his love for those who fear him. As far as the east is from the west, so far has he removed our transgressions from us."

If our Heavenly Father loves us and remembers our past sin no more, why would we give others the power to tell us differently? Will we continue to allow God's voice to be the loudest voice in our lives? Will we let His truths move us into our destiny?

In stepping into God's identity, it's quite possible there will be a transition that will involve a time of aloneness — just God and us. It's good. It's healthy. We must not fight it. There's also going to be a bombardment of comments and attacks regarding our deservedness and worth. We must abide. And most likely, there will be moments when others, and even us, question our royalty and significance. Fear not. We will refuse to believe such lies. We will trust in God's voice. He will have the loudest voice and we will take it to heart.

People often say, "I just need to find myself." They go on a long search attempting to figure out who they are.

They seek relationships, lifestyles, careers, experiences and knowledge. They attempt to define their identity in their own way and on their own terms. These falsehoods and delusions lead to more emptiness. The only way we can "find ourselves" is to find God. The only way to find ourselves is to discover our true identity in Christ.

The book of Genesis tells us we are made in the image of God and the entire Bible reinforces this truth. Truly, we are His image-bearers. Since this is fact, the only way an image-bearer can know who and what they are supposed to be, and do, is to know whose image they bear. It's impossible to know our identity if we don't know our Creator. We must know Him, His thoughts and His character to walk in our true identity. When we live in awe and wonder of God, and direct our mind to focus on who He is, then we discover our true identity. He's the very One who gives us our identity. Everything else is a false identity.

The Greek word, apostasia, is the English word apostasy. It means a falling away. More specifically, a falling away from the truth.[8] Truth is revealed to us through God's Word and when we fall away from His truth, we remove ourselves from the source of our true identity. Jeremiah 2:13 says, "My people have committed two sins: They have forsaken me, the spring of living water, and have dug their own cisterns, broken cisterns that cannot hold water."

The Jeremiah passage infers that there was an apostasia—a falling away from the source of truth and life. Removing ourselves from God leads us to create our own "source of life." If we remove ourselves from God, we will never be what we were intended to be. The Israelites chose to dig their own cisterns instead of relying on the pure spring of Living Water—the spring that was the very source of life and vitality. Instead, they chose to get water via runoff, etc. And to top it off, they tried to collect it with broken cisterns. Wow! What a picture. Why not just go to the source—to the spring of Living Water?

When we abide with our Father and allow Him to be the source of our existence, we will flourish and thrive. When we choose to live in a state of apostasia then we end up broken and empty, just like the Israelite cisterns. The Lord desires we flourish in the identity that He intended for us to live. It's through abiding in Christ, and living in His true identity, that we will silence the empty words of the accuser.

Revelation 12:10-11a proclaims,

> Then I heard a loud voice in heaven say: "Now have come the salvation and the power and the kingdom of our God, and the authority of his Messiah. For the accuser of our brothers and sisters, who accuses them before our God day and night, has been hurled down. They triumphed over him by the blood of the Lamb and by the word of their testimony;"

How do we silence the enemy's accusatory lies and live in our true identity?

It's through the power of what Jesus did on the cross and through the proclamation of our testimony of how God has stepped in and declared us forgiven, chosen, redeemed and free.

Remember the secretary bird from chapter three? When the enemy starts nipping at our heels and tries to convince us to be an image-bearer of the enemy, instead of God, or attempts to pull us back to the chicken coop, it's time to do the "secretary bird" stomp. We must crush his lies!

The New You

Jesus came to this earth to restore us into who He destined us to be. There is no power greater than Him. We must fight against the voices of our past. We must fight against the voices of today. We must fight the voices calling us into anything other than what our God has created for us to be. He desires for us to walk in freedom. He wants the "new you" to be fully alive!

It's time for us to leave our past behind. We are forgiven. He wants us to soar the way we were created and intended to soar. There's one God, one life and one you. We must live it to the fullest, in Him and through Him, for He alone makes *all things new!*

Reflection Questions and Action Steps:

1. Whose voice have you been listening to the loudest and why?

2. In what ways do you feel like you're scratching in the chicken pen, and in what ways do you feel like you're soaring like an eagle? Why?

3. Whose voice attempts to keep you away from living out your God-given identity, and what is it saying? In what ways can you block out that voice and listen only to God's?

4. How do you feel knowing that you are an image-bearer of God? How does knowing this fact change how you live?

5. Write a prayer of thankfulness to God and write out what your new identity in Christ looks like.

Afterword

As we close the pages of this book, my heart yearns for us all to continue to grow deeper in the love of the Father. Finding freedom and new life through His forgiveness is a journey. Our Heavenly Father desires for us to walk in complete wholeness through the power of Jesus Christ. He specializes in making *All Things New* – in every single area of our lives. Nothing is too difficult, and nobody is too far away, for His transformative power and restoration. What the enemy meant for evil in our lives can be radically turned around for our good. This is the nature of who our God is and what He specializes in. Romans 8:28 promises, "And we know that in all things God works for the good of those who love him, who have been called according to his purpose."

May we continue to walk into the person He created us to be. As the world relentlessly attempts to make us into its image, we will invite God to define us. He alone is given the authority to paint onto the canvas of our hearts and minds. He alone has all rights to restore our identity in Him.

I'm hearing the Holy Spirit cheer us on as we walk in His strength, wisdom and truth. I know His guidance and love will continue to lead us. I pray, in this next season of our lives, we experience the life-changing spiritual realities of Ephesians 3:16-21:

> *I pray that out of his glorious riches he may strengthen you with power through his Spirit in your inner being, so that Christ may dwell in your hearts through faith. And I pray that you, being rooted and established in love, may have power, together with all the Lord's holy people, to grasp how wide and long and high and deep is the love of Christ, and to know this love that surpasses knowledge—that you may be filled to the measure of all the fullness of God. Now to him who is able to do immeasurably more than all we ask or imagine, according to his power that is at work within us, to him be glory in the church and in Christ Jesus throughout all generations, for ever and ever! Amen.*

The Most Important Decision

One can never walk in true freedom apart from Jesus Christ. He alone is the Way, the Truth and the Life. Perhaps you've read the pages of this book but have never accepted Him for who He is and what He has done. There's a point in everyone's life where we must choose to accept His invitation. It's either a yes or no answer. There's no in between. We either accept Him or we reject Him. Let's look at what it means to choose Jesus Christ as our Lord and Savior.

FIRST – Why do we need a Savior?

Every single person walking on the face of the earth has sinned. Romans 3:23 says, "For all have sinned and fall short of the glory of God."

There isn't anyone who has lived a perfect life. Romans 3:10 says, "As it is written: 'There is no one righteous, not even one.'"

Everyone has sinned and the result of sin is death. Yet because of God's mercy and grace, we were provided a substitute for the penalty of death for our sin and His name is Jesus Christ. Romans 6:23 says, "For the wages of sin is death, but the gift of God is eternal life in Christ Jesus our Lord."

SECOND – Jesus is our Savior

Because we are imperfect beings, we cannot save ourselves from our sin which results in death. We need a Savior. Jesus, in His great love for us, took the penalty for our sin. Romans 5:8 says, "But God demonstrates his own love for us in this: While we were still sinners, Christ died for us."

It was God's unconditional love for us that provided a path for eternal life. John 3:16-18 says, "For God so loved the world that he gave his one and only Son, that whoever believes in him shall not perish but have eternal life. For God did not send his Son into the world to condemn the world, but to save the world through him. Whoever believes in him is not condemned, but whoever does not believe stands condemned already because they have not believed in the name of God's one and only Son."

There is only one way for us to be saved. There are not multiple methods for us to be redeemed from our sin and to have eternal life in heaven. We, as humans, cannot create a pathway of our own. There is only one way and there is only one true God. John 14:6 says, "Jesus answered, 'I am the way and the truth and the life. No one comes to the Father except through me.'"

Jesus became the substitute penalty for our sin so that we might be in right standing with God. Second Corinthians 5:21 states, "God made him who had no sin to be sin for us, so that in him we might become the righteousness of God."

THIRD – How do we accept Jesus as our Savior?

We must turn away from our sins. This is known as repentance. We must believe that Jesus Christ is our Lord and our Savior. We must confess our sins to God, believing He is faithful to forgive us. There isn't any amount of good works we can do that will bring our salvation. It is only by His grace we are saved.

Romans 10:9-10: "If you declare with your mouth, 'Jesus is Lord,' and believe in your heart that God raised him from the dead, you will be saved. For it is with your heart that you believe and are justified, and it is with your mouth that you profess your faith and are saved."

Romans 10:13: "Everyone who calls on the name of the Lord will be saved."

Acts 3:19: "Repent, then, and turn to God, so that your sins may be wiped out, that times of refreshing may come from the Lord."

Ephesians 2:8: "For it is by grace you have been saved, through faith – and this is not from yourselves, it is the gift of God."

1 John 1:9: "If we confess our sins, he is faithful and just and will forgive us our sins and purify us from all unrighteousness."

FOURTH – Next Steps

1. Say a commitment prayer to God.

2. Continue to learn more about God and how He wants you to live. A good place to start is to read the book of John in the Bible. Also, connect to a Bible-believing church.

3. Remind yourself of your new identity in Christ. His love for you will never end.

4. Commit to following God's standards in your everyday life.

Romans 8:1: "Therefore, there is now no condemnation for those who are in Christ Jesus."

1 John 3:1: "See what great love the Father has lavished on us, that we should be called children of God! And that is what we are!"

Colossians 3:1-3: "Since, then, you have been raised with Christ, set your hearts on things above, where Christ is, seated at the right hand of God. Set your minds on things above, not on earthly things. For you died, and your life is now hidden with Christ in God. When Christ, who is your life, appears, then you also will appear with him in glory."

PRAYER OF COMMITMENT

Prayer is simply talking with God. He loves authenticity and loves you to be real. To make a commitment and accept Jesus Christ as your Lord and Savor, it's as simple as confessing that you're a sinner, turning from your sinful ways to His righteous ways, believing that Jesus Christ is God, who died and was raised again so our sins would be forgiven, and asking Him to be the Lord of your life.

Pray and commit your life to God. There is no magic prayer, but God wants you to be genuine. He loves honesty and He loves commitment. Here is a sample prayer if you're unsure how to begin the conversation with God.

"Father God, I am in awe of your great love for me. I'm overwhelmed by your grace for me. I confess that I have sinned against you. Thank you for sending Jesus Christ to take the penalty for all my sin. I believe Jesus died on the cross for my sins and rose again so that I can live eternally with you. I commit my life to you and ask you to live in me. Again, thank you for your grace, mercy and overwhelming love for me. I love you and I commit to living the rest of my life for you and in you. In Jesus' name I pray, Amen."

1. Webb, Jonathan. "Lanky Bird's Killer Kick Quantified." BBC News, BBC, 25 Jan. 2016, https://www.bbc.com/news/science-environment-35400385.amp

2. Catafygiotu Topping, E. (n.d.). St. Photini, The Samaritan Woman. Orthodox Christian. http://www.orthodoxchristian.info/pages/photini.htm

3. Shepard, Leanna. "Sabina Wurmbrand: Radical Faithfulness, Beautiful Forgiveness." Revive Our Hearts, 3 Mar. 2016, https://www.reviveourhearts.com/blog/sabina-wurmbrand-radical-faithfulness-beautiful-fo/

4. Wurmbrand, Richard. In God's Underground. 2004.

5. C. S. Lewis (2003). "A Mind Awake: An Anthology of C. S. Lewis", p.148, Houghton Mifflin Harcourt

6. Ridler, Jason. "William Hull." The Canadian Encyclopedia, 8 Mar. 2011, https://www.thecanadianencyclopedia.ca/en/article/william-hull#WilliamHull

7. Staff, Site. "Hidden Masterpiece Discovered in Paris." KOAM, KOAM News, 26 Jan. 2019, https://www.koamnewsnow.com/hidden-masterpiece-discovered-in-paris/

8. "G646 - Apostasia - Strong's Greek Lexicon (KJV)." Blue Letter Bible, https://www.blueletterbible.org/lexicon/g646/kjv/tr/0-1/

About Author

Cheryl Braden is the co-founder of Legacy Incorporated, a nonprofit whose mission is to "build people, homes and schools around the world." Having served in church and para-church organizations, Cheryl is a dynamic communicator, transformational leader and human dignity advocate. Through the power of Jesus Christ, Cheryl is passionate about bringing life, healing and hope to individuals throughout the world.

For more information, visit www.CherylBraden.com.